The
Country Cottage
By George Ll. Morris
and Esther Wood

London : John Lane, The Bodley Head
New York: John Lane Company MDCCCCVI

VIEW OF A DAIRYMAN'S COTTAGE, WILSFORD, WILTSHIRE
Detmar Blow, Architect

Turnbull & Spears, Printers, Edinburgh.

Prefatory Note

IN sending out this book—its aim and object being to help those about to build a country cottage—we have the pleasure to thank those architects who have lent their drawings and photographs for the purposes of illustration. We have also to acknowledge our indebtedness to T. Hamlyn, Esq., of Messrs Bolding & Sons, who has helped us in the chapter on drainage, and whose practical knowledge on sanitary matters has been of great service.

40 FINSBURY SQUARE, E.C.

ANOTHER VIEW OF DAIRYMAN'S COTTAGE, WILSFORD, WILTSHIRE

Detmar Blow, Architect

Contents

vii

Contents

Contents

List of Illustrations

xi

List of Illustrations

List of Illustrations

xiii

List of Illustrations

List of Illustrations

List of Illustrations

The
COUNTRY COTTAGE

Chapter I.—*Introductory*

THE increasing demand for "a cottage in the country" is not confined to any one class of people, nor is it any longer significant of a humble mode of life. In olden days the dwellers in cottages were presumably the poor. Poets hymned the cottager as the man of toil, to whom the kindly parson ministered at his family festivals, and for whom the joy of living must depend largely on his relations with the squire. The cottage lass went barefoot from poverty rather than from choice, and her kindred accepted the hewing of wood and the drawing of water as the chief of the inevitable duties of life. Burns would have been amazed indeed to see the widely different kinds of pleasure, of occupation, and of social interest which go to make up the modern "Cotter's Saturday Night."

The problem, as it confronts the cottage-builder of to-day, is that cottages are wanted to suit almost every kind of domestic life that can be found in English society. The home of one of our younger princesses of the royal blood is a cottage of much smaller dimensions than the house of many a prosperous tradesman. Its

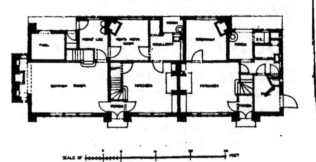

Ground Floor

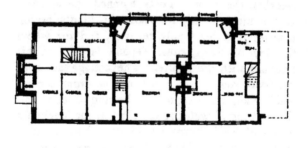

First Floor

COTTAGE IN SURREY

Messrs Dunn & Watson, Architects

elegance lies in what it fulfils of that simplicity and frugality of life—so much easier to conceive

2

than to live up to—which seem to be the last word of a true civilisation. On the other hand the crying need for inexpensive and sanitary cottages for labourers in country districts, and in the neighbourhood of mines, factories, etc., is one of the most genuine grievances of the social reformer. Capable and public-spirited officers of health, and members of urban councils, complain bitterly that their efforts are brought to a dead-lock by the apathy of those who ought at least to allow—if not to encourage—the building of simple and comfortable dwellings for the population on their land. Between these two demands—of the leisured person for a quiet and unpretentious dwelling, and of the labourer for a secure and permanent home, we have the rapidly growing desire of the ordinary man and woman, of average means, for a cottage in the country, where they may live and work in seclusion, or retire frequently from their work in town; where companionship may be enjoyed in a peaceful atmosphere, where the weary and convalescent may recruit their strength, and children be healthily and happily brought up.

Quite apart from the wholesome love of fresh air and natural scenery, and the much advocated "return to nature," which philosophers welcome in the movement towards country life, it is undoubtedly the symptom of a revolt on the part of many men and more women against the tyranny of the town house, with its standing problem of servants, and its inevitable burdens of cleaning and maintenance, entertaining on a scale which is "expected," and being more or less permanently "at home." Fortunately the modern householder has fairly shaken himself free of the old super-stitious dread of losing caste by moving into an obviously smaller dwelling; cycles and motors having completed the work of summer camps, house-boats, and shooting-boxes in fostering the taste for a permanent country retreat. The flat in town has been another valuable factor in the loosening of the old domestic chains. Whatever staff of servants may be necessary in a town house, both the flat and the cottage seem to promise a happy reduction of their number by the substitu-tion of day-servants for residential ones: and in the country it is generally enough to have one man or one maid permanently on the premises. Many housewives are already finding the system of day-service an immense relief from the constant charge of young girls removed from their own homes and families. Moreover the country cottage is not built to accommodate the separate *ménage* which a staff of resident servants involves; the chief consideration is that the early morning fires and hot water shall be provided either by the residual resident man or maid or by the incoming day-servant. The present generation has wit-nessed a quite revolutionary acceptance of this

4

A VIEW OF COTTAGES IN SURREY

Messrs. Dunn & Watson, Architects

mode of life. Fifty years ago, for anyone to
choose deliberately to live in a cottage when they
might live in a house was a vagary wholly unaccountable to the country mind. If we elected
to live in three rooms, it could be for no other
reason than because we could not afford six. To
do so in the teeth of a strong banking account
was to be charitably put down as eccentric, if not
insane; or to be dismissed from the social calendar
as " nobody."

Considering first the emigrants from the town,
rather than the country natives, we shall find their
reasons for desiring life in a cottage as diverse
as the people themselves. They will include the
man who goes to town because he cannot work in
the country, and the man who goes to the country
because he cannot work in town. Some of them
will have come there chiefly for solitude and
isolation; others for social recreation, and the
refreshment of a free and easy domestic life.
Some can pursue either their breadwinning
labours or their favourite hobbies equally well
in the home circle, and happy are they—though
their home circle may not always be so pleased
with the arrangement. Others prefer the sharp
dividing-line which circumstances or habits have
drawn between work and play, and like to go
home to a country cottage when their day's or
week's labour is finished, to enjoy the complete
change of surroundings, and the benefit of

sleeping and waking in pure air. These things
are mainly matters of temperament; to some the
country is an inspiration to work, to others it
is the place of all places where work is most
odious, and where the obvious duty is to loaf
and enjoy oneself. To others the country cottage
is chiefly desirable for the sake of bairns and
wife, and the man's own joy of it is a secondary
matter.

These, then, are the first questions for the
cottage-builder : for what sort of people is the
cottage intended, and what kind of life will they
want to live in it ? The nearer do they approach
the primitive labouring type — the farmer or
fisherman—the stronger is the need for a secure
and permanent homestead, inasmuch as the tenant
must perforce live and toil there in all weathers
and under all stress of good and bad seasons,
while the landlord, or any settler whose occupation does not bind him to that particular neighbourhood, has at least the alternative of spending
the most inclement periods elsewhere. The
cottager who stands for one of successive generations of toilers, rooted by many fibres to their
little patch of earth or shore, demands a dwelling
which shall at least secure him shelter, warmth,
and sanitary decency. The comforts of his home
are all the more important to him because he is
not free to leave it and look about for a more
convenient place.

ANOTHER VIEW OF COTTAGES IN SURREY

Messrs, Dunn & Watson, Architects

Such cottages have nearly always a resident housewife who lives and works mainly indoors, and who—however much she may appreciate good stoves and washing arrangements—does not hanker for all the modern labour-saving appliances which a less stable and domesticated household seeks eagerly when undertaking cottage life. The woman who has given her best years to professional work,—teaching, writing, pursuing an art or craft, or managing a business, is not— with the best will in the world—so muscularly strong or so quick at domestic labours as the woman who has done nothing else from her childhood; and the demand for a minimum of scrubbing, and indeed of any work that is really dirty and arduous, is a perfectly fair demand from the modern housewife of small means. The old-fashioned cottage dame, on the other hand, is apt, through sheer force of habit, to be over-zealous with her mop and pail; and the wise architect may, without thrusting new-fangled methods unduly upon her, make a vast difference to the extent and ease of her daily work if he so chooses. The most difficult part of his task will be to get rid of the semi-suburban villa ideals which are unhappily growing upon the labourer's wife, and to restore the honest comfort of the kitchen and living-room to the place of the stuffy little best parlour and the cramped and pretentious "hall." It should be obvious, for

7

instance, that when the cottage breadwinners come home frequently wet and always dirty, the first apartment in which they set foot should be of hospitable aspect, and with a brick or stone floor, where boots and outer garments can be removed, if not cleaned also, and which gives easy access to a bath. Nothing could be more incongruous than the return of the ploughboy to a home entered by a passage in which two can hardly pass, and where the wooden floor is set with foot-traps in carpet and linoleum, of the order "decayed-genteel."

The breaking down of these semi-suburban notions and replacing them by saner and sweeter ideas will probably come about when every other problem in cottage building has been solved. In the natural order of things, it should be just the reverse; the cottage beautiful should follow the better ideas; but nowadays it would seem as if we only saw beauty under direct provocation and only pressure of external circumstance would compel a workman to fling away his front parlour and his stuffed bird. Nothing is more depressing than to witness the eagerness with which the labourer or the mechanic comes out of a comfortable and homely old cottage to take up his residence in a brick box with a slate lid, and no cottager will go from one of these appalling modern structures into a pleasant, if rather inconvenient old one. In justice to him, we may

8

AN INTERIOR—THE COMMON ROOM, COTTAGES IN SURREY

Messrs. Dunn & Watson, Architects

UofM

urge that the new building is " up-to-date," and has the conveniences pertaining to a boxy parlour, a passage, a hall, and a hat-stand. Perhaps there is a bathroom also which he will use probably as a store, or his children to float paper ships. It is also built in accordance with rather silly bye-laws, and the housewife has the satisfaction of knowing her home is as good as the one next to it—a pleasure and joy her neighbour is seldom permitted to forget.

Again, there has been of late an enormous increase in the number of women who go out daily to some kind of employment, and who do this, not instead of, but in addition to, their ordinary work in the home. Many a modern cotter's wife combines in her own person the tasks of wage-earner and housekeeper, and being literally " on duty " all her waking hours. On such women the practical burdens of life seem to fall most heavily; and upon the details of their house-building—the arrangement of their rooms, the efficiency of their stoves, and the accessibility of coals and water—will depend very largely how far their condition approaches actual slavery. Housework, however hard, is immensely simplified when there is someone at home to keep the kitchen fire always going. The women employed indoors can arrange and vary that work as it suits them, and in the absence of the men-folk for ten or twelve hours, can sit down cheerfully to a meal of yesterday's scraps, with a "relish" in the form of bread and butter. But the outgoing day-labourer, factory-hand, or business woman finds the regular evening house-warming a much more difficult affair; and in the event of her delay, the home-coming male is faced with the revolutionary alternative of making his own tea and warming his own slippers. The architect who would find favour with this rapidly increasing class of tenants must provide the quickest means of getting fires and hot water, whereby the housewife just returned from work, and probably the most tired and hungry of the family, may appease the more or less polite clamourings of husband, children, and the visitor who invariably chooses that particular moment to drop in for a chat.

Questions of hospitality are not the least important to consider when migrating from town to country life. Those who are free to choose a district in which to take or build a cottage should clearly make up their minds as to how far they really desire isolation and freedom from the calls of social life. If quiet and retirement are the main objects of the change, they must avoid main roads and the easy access of stations, which invite surprise visits from injudicious friends. To artists and students, and indeed to anyone who has deliberately chosen a country life for purposes of seclusion and work, the difficulty of getting away from other people—especially when the pursuers

VIEW FROM INGLE-NOOK END, COTTAGES IN SURREY

Messsrs. Dunn & Watson, Architects

have motors and bicycles—is becoming seriously acute. The problem of so planning your rooms that at least one may be secure against interruption,

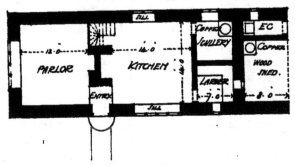

Ground Floor

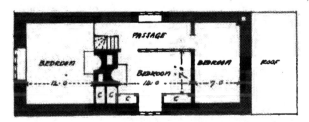

First Floor

PLANS OF A DAIRYMAN'S COTTAGE, WILSFORD, WILTSHIRE
Detmar Blow, Architect

and may not be invaded for any less cause than flood or fire, will have to be more fully considered by the modern cottager; inasmuch as neither argument nor demonstration will persuade anyone other than a brain-worker that the sounds of domestic life, half an hour's gossip, or a little music create any interruption at all.

For persons content with their own or each other's society, and not wanting quick or frequent communication with the outside world, there may be supreme advantages in a remote country spot, where only the carrier's cart or the postman's bugle bear witness to the persistence of civilisation at rare moments of the week or the day. On the other hand they must consider the questions of provisioning, of carriage from town or station, distance to shops and markets, etc., so that time wanted for work or rest will not be frittered away in endless tramps with bags and parcels; questions of the last train home if days in town are contemplated, and of the way from the station— whether by dark roads, fields, or commons where it is easy to lose one's way at night. A day-school for the children may also have to be thought of, as well as the personal service likely to be required from neighbours, and facilities for meeting and entertaining the visitors one really wishes to see.

In the matter of provisioning, the modern cottager will quickly rid himself of the illusion that country produce will be cheap and plentiful in proportion to his remoteness from London and large towns. Unless he is within reach of a good weekly market, or in a fruit-growing and pastoral country, and can deal directly with the growers and farmers, his supplies will be precarious indeed. Even by spending summer holidays in outlying districts, ideally picturesque to look at, many of us have discovered how grievous is the waste and mismanagement of local produce up and down the English countryside. Over the greater portion of the rural districts sung by poets for their gardens and orchards, fruit is a luxury reserved for Christmas Day, Bank holidays, and the gentry, and is rarely seen, save perhaps in a weekly pie, on middle-class tables. To the born Londoner, to whom the obtaining of any desired commodity, for domestic use, food, conveyance, or the toilet, has depended merely on its price, the limits which a country cottage will set upon his personal habits may offer many surprises. His neighbours may appear to him barbarians in their indifference and ignorance concerning things he believes to be necessaries of life, but it will be wise not to ride roughshod over country prejudices, nor to assert too aggresively a mode of life which he considers superior to theirs. He will probably find the happy mean in a cheerful independence, a kindly recognition of friendly advances, and a good-humoured confession of eccentricity where habits necessary to his comfort are such as they cannot understand.

CHAPTER II.—*Site and Soil*

"HOW much will it cost?" is naturally the first question asked when the desire for a cottage in the country begins to resolve itself into definite proposals and plans. For the purposes of this little handbook it may be assumed that a cottage is a building whose total cost should not exceed £1000. It may be brought within £300, or even lower, by methods presently to be discussed. Many tempting schemes lie within a couple of hundred pounds beyond the maximum here given, but we may take it that the great majority of those who contemplate building a cottage of their own have set themselves, roughly speaking, a limit of three figures, and are anxious to know how much they may reasonably expect to do for such a sum.

Questions of land tenure, which must first be decided, hardly come within the scope of discussion here; but over and above these there are certain restrictions as to what may or may not be built on any given estate, which are in the hands of the local authorities, and may vary somewhat according to the good sense and discretion of the governing bodies. The local byelaws, in fact, present one of the greatest difficulties with which the intending builder has to deal.

Frequently they are arbitrary and wasteful in their carrying out, and destructive of the artistic principles on which the designer has based his work. The regulation, for instance, that all ground floor and first rooms must be at least nine feet high is not only unnecessary but wasteful in a small cottage. It fails of its presumably hygienic purpose in workmen's dwellings, because, although the English labourer has no love of fresh air, his front door can be kept open during the greater part of the year, and in winter the extra height of the room entails more artificial heating —a matter of considerable moment to the cottager. It also increases the expense, and allows the architect little opportunity to attempt any new treatment. Again, the use of thatch for roofing is now forbidden in some districts where it was formerly customary, and thus one of the most beautiful of local traditions is wantonly crushed out. In other cases, cottages built of weather boarding lined with felt and wood, having only the foundations and chimneys of brick, have been condemned and removed on the plea of unsuitable materials. The objection to thatch and weather boarding, on the ground of their inflammable nature, might be reasonable enough in a crowded district, but it is pointless in the case of a detached country cottage; and the recent formation of a society for the express purpose of fighting, and if possible abolishing, such bye-laws as are really harsh and useless, bears witness to the extent to which the grievance is felt by those who are trying to meet the demand for cottages in a practical way, and of moderate cost.

To anyone with no experience of building in the country, this active opposition to certain bye-laws of a vexatious nature may seem to open the way to workmanship of a flimsy and undesirable kind. It is, however, extremely doubtful whether the abolition—or at any rate the considerable modification of these restrictions—(relating to the heights of rooms, thickness of walls, sizes of windows and timber, and the specification of materials) will bring about the bad results which have followed upon their strict administration. If any improvement is to be made on country cottage building, the most irrelevant of these ill-considered regulations must either be done away with altogether, or drawn up by a responsible authority with some regard for the difference between town and country life. We find, for instance, that it is impossible in the country to erect a cottage in the middle of a 500-acre field except by complying with all the regulations, while in London, provided you give a certain space all round your building, you can build very much as you please. Another serious objection—raised by Mr J. St Loe Strachey in the *County Gentleman*—is the check it puts upon the invention of new materials.

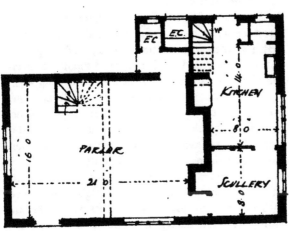

Ground Floor

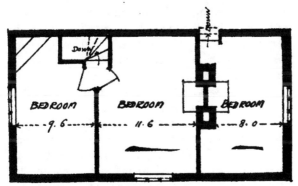

First Floor

COTTAGE AT WALLCOTT, GAP BACTON, NORFOLK

Detmar Blow, Architect

B

At the present time, if an architect or manufacturer were to discover a material which would enable a cottage to be built for a hundred pounds (£100), he would find it very difficult to make use of it throughout the greater part of England.

Much as we may covet for our modern homes the durability and substantial look of ancient cottages, conditions will arise in modern life that make these characteristics unattainable; and there seems no reason why cottages built in a sheltered place, to meet an immediate and urgent need, should not be of an altogether lighter structure, so long as they make no pretensions to be any more solid and costly than they are. There is a vast difference between jerry-building — which means something built for sale and for show— and the construction of a dwelling-place in common and homely materials, which are put together with judgment and skill, and are in themselves sound, cleanly, and reliable as far as they go. In fact the cottage builder of limited means is far more likely to get a beautiful result if he builds thus simply and frankly according to his needs than if he started out to build in any given "style," following any ancient or modern examples that appealed to his eye when he saw them, perhaps in totally different surroundings.

A cottage, to be beautiful, must be planned to suit the life of the tenant and to harmonise outwardly with the landscape on which it is placed.

VIEW OF A COTTAGE AT WALLCOTT GAP, BACTON, NORFOLK
Detmar Blow, Architect

Site and Soil

Computations of cost will very soon make it clear
that a building on an exposed site will need
firmer foundations and greater stability than the
cot on a sunny hillside or in the covert of a
woodland vale. Geological formations also will
generally yield hard ground on peaks, cliffs,
downs, and upland plains, and comparatively soft
ground in dales and valleys, providing together
with the primal soil the materials with which to
build. This unity of the very stuff of the house
with its site and surroundings is the keynote of
beauty in the architecture of the countryside.
Looking into the best English traditions of
cottage-building we find, without exception, that
the most satisfactory results have been obtained
where the builders have recognised and preserved
most faithfully this natural tie between the cottage
and the soil. The building should never give the
impression of a ready-made thing taken out of a
workshop and suddenly set down upon the site.
Rather it should hug the ground as if it loved it,
as if it were born of the very spirit of the place.
To ignore that spirit in over-anxiety to be
original, and to build, as it were, "out of one's
own head," is very much as if a violinist should
tune his instrument to any pitch that seemed good
to him, quite irrespective of the pitch adopted by
the orchestra with which he is going to play.

A few of our modern architects have admirably
fulfilled these conditions, and have planted really

beautiful cottages along the ancient highways and byeways of remote country districts. Such men

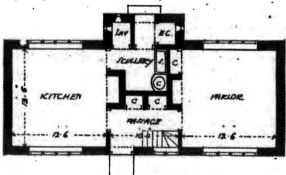

Ground Floor

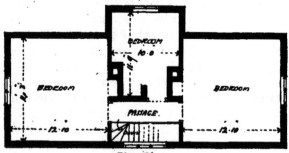

First Floor

PLANS OF ROEHAMPTON LODGE
Detmar Blow, Architect

as Mr Phillip Webb and Mr E. E. Lutyens in Surrey, Sussex, and Essex, Mr Detmar Blow in the characteristic flint districts of Wiltshire, and

VIEW OF A COTTAGE IN BRADGATE PARK, LEICESTERSHIRE

Built by Detmar Blow & E. Gimson, Architects

Site and Soil

Mr Guy Dawber in the Gloucestershire wolds, have shown us how an architect who is an artist may respect and preserve in his work the traditions of the place without merely imitating or forfeiting anything vital to his individuality. In such hands a human habitation may crown the most perfect landscape in a dignified and quite poetic way. There need be no provocation for the plaint of the old pietist contemplating Nature, "where every prospect pleases and only man is vile." Unfortunately the facilities of modern transit have made it easy for the vandal to bring together all manner of incongruous materials, and to use them on a site where they will never look at home; and such enterprises have gradually broken up the old and sound tradition that the substance of a house should be of the local materials—stone, flint, and slate being used in the districts that yield them, timber in a well-wooded country, bricks and tiles on a clay soil, thatch in the agricultural counties, and so on. In following these principles we discover how closely the domestic architecture of a nation is bound up with its political and social conditions, and how disastrous—even from the artistic standpoint—may be the de-forestation of large tracts of land, the neglect of what might be profitable country, and the destruction or decay of pastoral life.

It may be urged at this point that nobody

should undertake to make a new home for himself in the country without first spending some time in the proposed place to make sure that it suits his health and temperament. Occasional week-ends are not a sufficient test, especially for persons whose health is susceptible to differences of climate. A great deal was said and written a few years ago on the question of soil in relation to health, tending to the general disparagement of clay and the recommendation of chalk and gravel. These broad generalisations are now as much discredited as the old classification of districts as "bracing" or "relaxing,"—the latter to be universally shunned and the former sought after. We are now discovering, not only that different constitutions are suited by many different kinds of soil and air, but that personal idiosyncrasy is a much more real and unaccountable thing than we formerly reckoned it. Nobody knows exactly why one person is immensely benefited by a particular place, while another, apparently subject to precisely the same ailments, can never thrive in it. He who goes forth to recruit his health in a new country home must decide for himself that the chosen place suits him, not because he has been told that it *ought* to suit him, but simply because he finds himself well and happy there. Moreover, the treatment of weakly persons and invalids as regards climate, has been completely revolutionised within the last fifty years. Consumptive and bronchitic patients, for instance, who were once sent to warm and sheltered resorts to lounge in cushioned bath-chairs and stuffy lodgings, are now despatched to the mountain-tops to sleep in the open air and take regular exercise. We have learnt also that physical treatment and surroundings are not the only—and some would say not the chief—factors in convalescence, and that the attuning of the inner man to the beauty of the earth and sky plays no small part in the restoration of the harmony which we know as bodily health and vigour.

We have said that the expense of building will depend partly on the position of the site, its exposure to weather, and the nature of the soil. The higher it is, the more need (as a rule) for the walls to be solid and the foundations strong; and the more likely is the ground to be hard to dig and the materials difficult to convey. From the point of view of the building itself the ideal foundation is gravel. Rock stands next, but is expensive in the working. The chief things to be avoided are a wet, sandy soil, and clay veined with running sand—a sure cause of cracked walls and ceilings. Stiff clay makes a fair foundation, but generally needs a depth of three or four feet for the excavations. On the other hand, a fine and commanding site often pays well for a little extra expense in its advantages of air and scenery. But for residents going frequently to town it may be a serious item whether the road to the station be uphill or down; for however much one may dislike the uphill climb on coming home, it can at least be taken at leisure; while a climb to the station generally involves an exhausting, if not a dangerous, rush for the train.

Another important consideration is whether the garden is to play an important part in the cottager's life. In finding a climate for himself, he may be counting on the joys of cultivating his garden—only to find that nothing will grow in it. Granting, however, a favourable soil, the possibilities of the garden should certainly be reckoned with in deciding the way in which the house is to be set. The fruit-lover will aim at the largest area of sunny wall consistent with the needs of the dwelling. Possibly a tennis lawn will be allowed for, and if possible a sunny verandah and a paved and sheltered place where dirty work may be done out of doors. All available sunlight and wind-shelter will be secured for the best flower-beds. The building should look well from all sides, and it is a mean economy to use inferior materials at the back than those of the frontage. The comfort of the dwelling as to its position and aspects should never be sacrificed to its appearance from the street or other approaches. No matter how odd it may appear to the conventional eye to see the cottage set corner-wise or at a different angle from its neighbours, it is far better

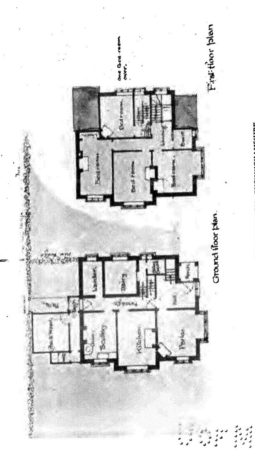

Ground floor plan.

First floor plan

One Bed room over.

PLANS OF A COTTAGE FARM, BUCKINGHAMSHIRE
C. Spooner, Architect

to have it so than to allow any of the rooms to face due north. The chief care should be to get all possible sunlight into the dwelling. In England we need never be afraid that any part of the house will get too much sun—unless it be the larder; and this should face the north or north-east. The immense value of the morning sun in bedrooms (unless disliked by habitually late risers), and also in the breakfast room, can hardly be overrated, and it is nearly always better to give the afternoon sun to rooms occupied later in the day.

CHAPTER III.—*Grouping*

THE water supply is another important matter to be looked into before a final decision is made upon the site. The sinking of a well may be an expensive operation, and in any case the tenant should know clearly what the water is that he proposes to depend upon, whether it is absolutely secure from contamination, and whether the supply is ever likely to fail him. Water from a stream, even in the remotest districts, is open to the double objection that it may fail in a long drought, or become polluted. In this respect even spring water is not infallible. Moreover, the quality of the water as a drinking supply, quite apart from its freedom from actual poisons, is a matter for serious consideration. Many invalids find their ailments much aggravated by the constant use of water in which large quantities of iron and lime are present—a condition on which no amount of filtering will have very much effect. Moreover, the idea that hard water contains much bone-building material, advantageous to young people, is pretty well exploded. Many persons recommend the boiling of all water used for drinking and cooking, and this plan no doubt is excellent, unless rainwater can be secured absolutely clean.

VIEW OF A COTTAGE FARM, BUCKINGHAMSHIRE
C. Spooner, Architect

But if we are to depend on servants for the duty of boiling the water daily, we may be practically certain that it will never be done.

The man who sets out to build a cottage after his own heart, is sure to be beset by the multitude of counsellors with whom wisdom is supposed to lie. We shall be fortunate if we escape with the brief advice of Mr Punch to those about to marry. More probably our friends will describe to us at great length all the disastrous building experiments they ever heard of. And then, however carefully we may select our architect, and explain to him what sort of cottage we are seeking, the speculating builder will come upon the scene and offer us a cheaper and apparently more desirable thing. Unfortunately, his claim will be plausible enough at first sight. He will undoubtedly be able to build *in his own way* a cottage of the required size more cheaply than we could do it with our architect's aid. Not that the well-built cottage always costs more in actual materials. On the contrary, a capable architect will often be able to effect a great saving, both of materials and labour, by various small sacrifices and contrivances, which the man of routine would think beneath his notice. This, however, means time and trouble, forethought, experience, and practical skill; and if we employ a qualified architect, these are precisely the things for which we pay. The wise client will perceive that in such a bargain he secures what the ordinary

27

builder could not give him. The latter will never even try to give us what we want. It would not pay him to do so.

It must also be remembered that a single cottage is a luxury. It is always relatively cheaper to build in rows or pairs. Under our present civilization, a single thing honestly and plainly made as the owner wants it, is far more costly and difficult to get than a set of a dozen things made after one pattern, and this applies as much to a cottage as to a deal table. The detached cottage is an individual thing. It may escape the obvious temptation to be eccentric; but it will certainly need individual treatment in design. It takes a more luxurious form in the bungalow, spreading itself over a larger area and dispensing with stairs. It will, therefore, preferably be erected where bye-laws are reasonably elastic, and land is cheap. But in any case the single cottage should be homely, restful, and as far as bye-laws will permit, generally built in low, spreading lines.

When building cottages in pairs or rows, the obvious comfort of a sound-proof party wall should be one of the first considerations. It will entail extra expense, but some sacrifice should certainly be made to secure it, considering what it means to be at the mercy of musical or loudly devotional neighbours, or children kept very much indoors. A case recently occurred in which a quiet family of students were compelled to turn out of their

semi-detached cottage because the next door neighbour's child, clad in boots heavy enough to negotiate
a snowdrift, was allowed to run incessantly up and
down the length of the ground-floor passage,
during what seemed to be the whole of its waking
hours.

Quadrangles have many practical advantages,
and not the least is that they afford a place
where children may safely be sent out to play.
Of course the privacy of one's own garden is
forfeited, and much will depend upon how far the
social standards and interests of the residents are
alike, and will reconcile them to a common play-
ground for the little ones. In any case, one can
be just as neighbourly, or just as exclusive, in a
small street as in a quadrangle ; the disadvantages
of the former, as regards children, being the
danger of traffic and of straying beyond bounds,
and the chance of a little more dirt. The excellent plan of a roof-garden, which serves also
to dry clothes, is not often available for buildings
on the cottage scale.

The social difficulty solves itself to some extent
in a model village of the kind where the inhabitants, by daily contact in common dining-rooms
and recreative clubs, become somewhat " broken
in" to communal life. Robert Owen long ago
urged the plan of building cottages in groups or
squares, with a public kitchen or mess-room for
labour-saving purposes ; and though it is doubtful

whether the ordinary cottager (at all events on the female side) is ready for this readjustment of domestic machinery, it may fairly be hoped that some such economic development will occur, and that the industrial colony is a step in that direction. Probably, if anything is to be achieved in this country in the way of garden cities, they will have to grow up similarly from the industrial changes of the time. The question of how far the daily labours of the home will ultimately be lightened by common kitchens and warehouses is a very interesting and problematic one. Upon the answer to it must depend the scheme of domestic life for the next generation, and with it the development of cottage architecture.

We have already referred to Robert Owen's scheme, and to the advantages of such industrial colonies as Port Sunlight, but a still wider application of these ideas is possible for the professional and middle-class man. There seems no reason to suppose that the city man would not welcome the formation of a country cottage colony in a neighbourhood conveniently situated for getting to and fro from town. A scheme, neither too regular nor affectedly picturesque, well planned and arising out of the peculiarities of site and place, might be beautiful, or again, it might not. It would depend largely whether those responsible were capable of choosing the architects. We can imagine that such a colony, with blocks or single cottages designed by Mr Lethaby, Mr Lutyens, Mr Troup, Mr Guy Dawber, Mr Geo. Jack, Mr Detmar Blow, and others of a sympathetic spirit, would be a success; on the other hand, a colony by * * * * *, it is almost needless to say, would be a chaos of brick, slates, and model dwellings, such as we all know and wish we did not.

In considering the building of cottages in groups or large numbers, and the forming up of streets and terraces, we are confronted with one of the most interesting developments of modern life—the industrial colony or "model village," built to accommodate the fairly fixed population depending on a large factory employing many workers. The efforts towards the systematic housing of day-labourers near their industrial centre, undoubtedly leaves much to be desired, and have been held up to the just scorn of reformers. They are generally ugly, barrack-like, and comfortless. This reproach, however, can fairly be said to be partially removed by such industrial colonies as Messrs Cadbury's at Bourneville, and Messrs Lever's at Port Sunlight, not to speak of others of recent growth, the study of which will repay those interested in the social aspects of architecture.

CHAPTER IV.—*Plans*

HAVING fixed upon our site, the next decision to be made is the shape of the house to be put upon it, and the materials of which it is to be built. Broadly speaking, the choice lies between six types, as follows:—

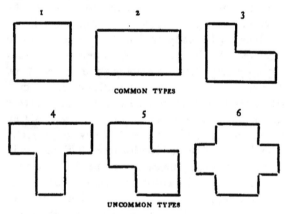

COMMON TYPES

UNCOMMON TYPES

These are here given in the order of their cost; that based on a square being naturally the simplest and most economical. Any variation from this means a more complex roof, and the multiplication of outer walls, and here additional expense comes in. The L shape, however, is often convenient,

32

especially on low-lying and sheltered sites It is
a plan much favoured by Mr C. F. A. Voysey,

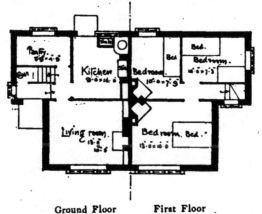

Ground Floor　　First Floor

COTTAGES AT ALDERTON, SUFFOLK
(These are the plans of Cottages illustrated on title-page)

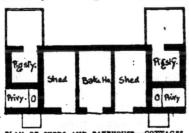

PLAN OF SHEDS AND BAKEHOUSE—COTTAGES
AT ALDERTON, SUFFOLK
C. Spooner, Architect

and includes some of his most successful work.
It is apt to be too cold for exposed places, unless,

in the planning, the chimneys come naturally at both ends as well as at the central juncture, and this is rather an extravagant, not to say wasteful, arrangement. It is a general rule that the chimney shaft should be the centre or focussing point of

COTTAGES AT ALDERTON
C. Spooner, Architect

the house, and the colder the district, the more carefully should the various rooms be disposed around that central heat. We all know the winter discomforts of a long and narrow room; if the fire-place is at one end, the other is never warm, if in the middle, both are cold equally. In small cottages, of which one room and a passage form the full width, the main chimney often gets driven to one side, and forms an important feature of the

VIEW OF COTTAGES IN SUSSEX, FROM THE GARDEN
C. Spooner, Architect

exterior, as in Surrey, Kent, and Sussex, where this became the almost universal plan. Here arises the obvious economy of building cottages of such a size in pairs, but, on the other hand, the outline of a little cottage flanked by its own chimneys, broadly and simply treated, is distinctly pleasing to the eye. Chimney-shafts not in the middle of the building should, if possible, occupy the wall that gets the least sun. Cupboards for clothes and linen, and stores to be kept dry, should be close beside them, or against a sunny wall.

We have already urged the importance of preserving what the late J. D. Sedding so aptly called the "*localness*" of English art. Just as we find in travelling about the country, the various dialects succeeding one another as we pass from each county to the next, till the remoter natives of north and south seem to be speaking quite a different tongue, so in our country-side architecture, every district has inherited its own forms of expression, and a feeling of respect for these should restrain the modern architect from dumping down a cottage of "marked" originality upon a peaceful hillside. Indeed, the discreet client will avoid altogether an architect who prides himself on things "quaint," "picturesque," and "artistic"; knowing that sound and straightforward building, whether old or new, must carry beauty in its train, and local traditions will be found to bear a true relation to the needs of the case.

From the æsthetic standpoint, there is no reason
why a row of cottages should be any less beautiful than the single dwelling, or degenerate into
the dull, monotonous line of " square brick boxes
with slate lids," which William Morris so ab-
horred. To get a pleasing diversity in the
frontage and in the general plan involves a little
more forethought and skill in the design, but
not necessarily much extra expense. A covered
passage or right of way between the houses, or
an archway to let vans into a yard, can generally
be treated in a pleasant manner, instead of
making the immediate surroundings look sordid
and slummy because of them. The country
cottages of Mr Walter Cave afford some delightful instances of diversified frontages, and the
breaking up of small terraces in a convenient and
agreeable way.

In this diversity of treatment adopted by Mr
Walter Cave, there is of course a danger—that
in the hands of a less capable designer, it could
easily degenerate into meaningless eccentricity and
restlessness. To be "picturesque" and "original"
very often covers a multitude of sins, and frequently an excuse for incompetence and want of
thought, and it is therefore well that neither
architects nor those intending to build should be
afraid of some monotony: it is, after all, a good
characteristic, and a part of fine architecture,
whether it be of the cottage or cathedral.

A COTTAGE IN SUSSEX. VIEW FROM THE GARDEN

C. Spooner, Architect

CHAPTER V.—*Drainage*

BYE-LAWS as to the drainage and foundations of a dwelling-house are very properly stringent. On other points they may be arbitrary and vexatious, and indeed are so in many districts ; but few would wish to see them relaxed where they relate to matters of life and death, not only to the tenant but to his neighbours. A foul drain, a neglected cesspool, may poison and devastate a whole country-side. A famine of water is in many ways more disastrous than a famine of food, and is much more intimately bound up with questions of private building and public works. The individual tenant may perhaps claim the right to expose himself to risks of fire, cold, damp, and other personal dangers; but he must not be allowed to breed diphtheria without a protest, or to contaminate the local water supply in such a manner as to convey typhoid to a neighbour a quarter of a mile away. It is in drainage and water arrangements, more than in any other matter, that the inhabitants of a street, town, or village are made to suffer for each other's sins, and there is no question that should appeal more strongly to the social conscience, as involving duties equally binding upon the private tenant and the governing body whom he elects to control the public works of the neighbourhood.

Many able sanitarians declare that our whole system of the disposal of sewage is radically wrong, and that what is now wastefully thrown out to sea would, if properly applied to land cultivation, so enormously improve the fertility of the soil as to solve one of the agricultural problems of this country. Undoubtedly there is great truth in this contention, and the direct application of sewage to the land should be encouraged wherever it is practicable. In these matters, however, there is no room for makeshift or compromise; and though a country cottage may sometimes conveniently allow of the more rational and profitable dealing with sewage than by merely getting rid of it, still it cannot be too strongly urged that when the drainage system, commonly applied to town houses, is adopted in a country cottage, it needs to be thoroughly and scientifically done. The fact of a house standing in beautiful country air will not make it any the less dangerous to live in if the waste-pipes and soil-pipes are improperly trapped and ventilated, or insufficiently flushed with water in the course of daily use. It surely should not be too much to expect that the architect and the builder should have at least a sound general knowledge of modern appliances and methods of drainage, and how to adapt them to the particular needs of small houses, where economy of mechanism has to be considered. However important the æsthetic side of house-

vhole
ically
rown
land
:ility
ural
e is
rect
en-
1ese
ke-
try
:he
1ge
be
:m,
n a
:nd
ng
he
nd
or
of
to
ld
·n
:o
s,
:d.
3e-

A COTTAGE ON THE QUANTOCKS, SOMERSET

C. Spooner, Architect

building, the question of health and sanitary convenience must take precedence of all others. Cottages, however modest on cost, "ought to have this redeeming feature about them, however ugly, ill-designed, or badly constructed they may be—namely, that they are *safe to live in* as far as the internal drainage and plumbing are concerned."

On the other hand, it is only reasonable to ask that the householder himself should have a clear understanding of the main principles on which his dwelling is drained and supplied with water, and should be able to keep an intelligent look-out for defects and accidents, and the consequences of necessary wear and tear. It is obvious, of course, that the flow of water should be regular and full, that apparent stoppages of pipes should be at once attended to, and that the clean water supply should be kept wholly separate from the outlets of waste. Nor should it be necessary to warn the tenant that a boiler will burst, with disastrous results, if allowed to empty itself and be heated by a fire before fresh cold water runs in; or to teach him the simple ways of protecting his pipes from frost, such as by covering them properly or emptying when necessary. It is not always easy, however, to detect the dangers arising from errors of construction for which the plumber and builder are to blame. We are apt to think that all is safe so long as no bad smell is present. But a very little knowledge will show us how easy it is for

dangerous waste to accumulate and the air of the
house to be contaminated unknown to the householder. Hence the importance of making all
traps, joints, and connections easily accessible for
periodic inspection.

Trapping and ventilating are the two chief
means employed to prevent the accumulation and
leakage of vitiated air in the neighbourhood of the
drain-pipes. A trap is practically an automatic
water-door into a soil-pipe or waste, so contrived,
by a backward twist in the pipe, as to make a
temporary seal of fresh water every time the drain
is flushed, which lies in the trap until the next
flushing.

In districts where it is possible to obtain a
connection with a main sewer, the drains from the
cottage will be arranged to discharge into it and
at a point as near as possible to the boundary wall
or fence. An intercepting trap must be provided.
This trap prevents the vitiated air from the sewer
entering the house drain. Drain-pipes should be
of glazed stone-ware, or of heavy cast-iron coated
with Dr Angus Smith's solution and laid on a bed of
concrete 6 inches thick, with a fall of about 1 in
40. In jointing up the pipes care should be taken
that they are made perfectly water-tight, and
before the drain is covered in, it should be tested
by being plugged and filled with water. For the
proper cleaning of the drain from time to time,
manholes or inspection chambers should be placed

ANOTHER COTTAGE ON THE QUANTOCKS, SOMERSET

C. Spooner, Architect

U of M

THE KITCHEN IN A COTTAGE ON THE QUANTOCKS, SOMERSET

C. Spooner, Architect

in convenient positions fitted with air-tight covers. It is essential that all junctions and connections are arranged to join main drain in a chamber. On the house side of intercepter, there should be a fresh air inlet and a ventilation pipe at least 4 inches in diameter at head of drain. In cases where the w.c. is on the first floor the soil-pipe must be carried up well above eaves, full bore to act as drain ventilator. As this is rather unsightly, a better plan is to take the pipe up to the eaves level, and then continue it inside the roof and bring it out again at the ridge, finished with a wire guard to prevent birds building in it. Waste-pipes from the bath, lavatories, or sink, should discharge over a trap or gulley with open grating and under no circumstances must they discharge direct into the drain.

Soil-pipes, that is pipes from w.c.'s and slop sinks can be of heavy lead or strong cast-iron, and fixed outside building. If they are of lead, the connection to drain should be made with a brass tail-piece and cement joint to drain and a soldered joint to lead pipe; it is important that this should be carefully done, or it may become a source of danger. If the pipes are of cast-iron, the joints are made with yarn and caulked with blue lead perfectly tight, and not as frequently carried out with putty or red and white lead, which soon perishes, and then the joints will leak.

In probably the majority of districts the bye-laws

deal with these matters, but the above few rules will be found in general agreement with practically all. The rain-water drains will be kept quite separate from the soil drain and arranged to discharge into cistern, underground tank or butt.

One of the most picturesque features of the old-fashioned cottage was its rain-water butt. The neglect and gradual disuse of this excellent institution is greatly to be deplored, not merely on æsthetic grounds, but because of the immense value of clean rain-water from the hygienic and sanitary point of view, not to speak of its practical convenience in lightening the labour of the laundress and the domestic "washer-up." No one who has once realised what is gained in health and comfort by taking a little trouble to secure a soft-water supply for the household, either by filtering rain-water or boiling (or distilling the earth supply), will ever return willingly to the hard solace of the pump or tap.

The position of rain-water butts should of course be carefully considered with a view of protecting them from soil. It is not desirable that the contents should filter through clogged and untended roof-gutters, forsaken bird's-nests, or drifts of soot. But with a little care in the arrangement and protection of the watercourses, combined with suitable storage, a more or less constant supply can generally be had.

In cases where there is no main sewer a cess-

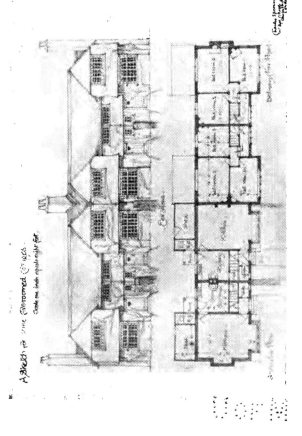

PLANS AND SKETCH ELEVATIONS, FIVE-ROOMED COTTAGES

C. Spooner, Architect

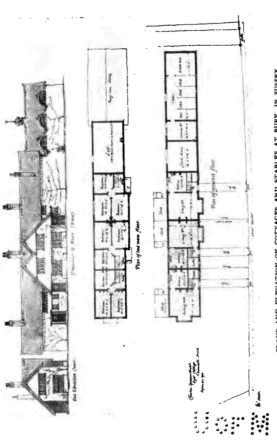

Plan of first main floor.

PLANS AND ELEVATION OF COTTAGES AND STABLES AT BURY, IN SUSSEX

C. Spooner, Architect

pool will be necessary, and care should be taken in the selection of its position. It should be as far from the cottage as can be conveniently arranged, and constructed to suit the requirements of sub-soil, and so that it may be emptied and cleaned without being a nuisance. Generally it will be found best to construct it circular in plan and of 9-inch brickwork, cement-coated inside with cement and sand to make water-tight. An iron air-tight cover should be provided. The overflow pipe and also the inlet to cesspool should have a bend fixed on so that the surface is not disturbed, allowing bacterial action to take place. If this is done, the cleansing of cesspool will not be required so often as the solids more or less disappear. The disposal of the overflow must be governed by circumstances, but it is best carried out by sub-irrigation—that is by perforated pipes 2 feet underground. As it is not always possible to do this owing to the ground being of clay or waterlogged, the overflow must be omitted and the cesspool made large enough for its purpose. The size of pipes will vary, but as a general rule the following will be best :—

Intercepting trap, 4 inches × 6 inches.
Drain-pipes, 4 inches.
Soil and ventilation pipes, 3½ inches or 4 inches.
Waste-pipes, 1½ inches or 2 inches.

It is not advisable to have the pipes too large

as they do not get properly cleaned by the flow of water, and leave deposit in the pipes which, on becoming decomposed, causes smells and noxious

Ground Floor. (Three Bedrooms on First Floor)

COTTAGE AT CHISLEHURST

E. J. May, Architect

gases. The vertical waste-pipe from upstair fittings should be carried above eaves as ventilation, so that a current of air is continually passing through the grating of gulley and going out at the top. The outlet should have a wire dome grating

similar to that used for soil-pipe. In choosing
such fittings as baths, lavatories, and w.c.'s for a
country cottage, it should be borne in mind how
difficult it is to get repairs properly executed in
the country, and for this reason should be of as
simple a character as possible, so that the repairs
necessary may consist generally only of a new
washer that can be done by the cottage owner
himself. The best and simplest form of w.c.
is a pedestal, there are several good forms in the
market, and these, without attempts at decoration
are generally the best for appearance. The basin
should have a good flushing rim, and the back of
the pan vertical and the seal of the trap not less
than 2 inches, and capable of clearing itself with a
2-gallon flush. The flushing cistern of the
" Syphon" description is the best to use, with a
capacity of 2 or 3 gallons and as quiet as possible.
A great number of these cisterns are noisy and
objectionable. The inlet to this cistern should be
of sufficient bore to fill it in 60 seconds or less;
nothing is more exasperating and objectionable
than to have one that takes 15 or 20 minutes.
If the cistern is enclosed, the enclosure must be so
arranged that the cistern can easily be got at for
repairs.

There is perhaps no question on which public
opinion has changed more completely during the
last half century than the question of baths.
Those days are past of which a cynic said that it

was the custom of the English to wash the face and hands daily, and the back of the neck and the feet (with due precautions against taking cold) on Saturday nights. Even the general acceptance of the bath as "an excellent thing for those who can afford it," has now given place to the more rational view that the dirtier a man's employment is, the more imperative a bath becomes, not only for his own health and decency, but also for the comfort of his neighbours.

Further, it is a mistake to suppose that baths, or even bath-rooms, are a heavy additional expense to the dwelling. They often are so when added as an after thought, but they need not be so when provided for in the original plans. To begin with, it will of course be a great saving of expense if the bathroom is placed on the ground floor. No water-pipes need then be carried upstairs, and the whole of the fittings, including bath, boiler, sinks, and all sanitary conveniences subject to the plumber's craft, can be grouped together within a few yards. Care should be taken, however, that each part of the water-supply is separately accessible, and that one member of the household is not kept waiting for a quick wash or a jug of water while another monopolises the room containing the lavatory basin or tap. For the same reason it is a bad practice to put the private conveniences in the bathroom, as is so often done in small suburban houses, where a great deal of needless delay and annoyance is caused by the apartment being occupied for the one purpose when wanted for the other.

Lavatories and baths are open to a wide choice, but it is suggested that if wood enclosures are fitted round them, they may become a receptacle for dust and rubbish. The independent form is perhaps the best. The cottage builder should see that the supply valves are of good quality and of the screw down pattern, as these are easiest repaired. The waste valves should be large and with proper traps.

The scullery sink may be of strong stone-ware either buff or white-glazed, and carried on brick or stone cortels or iron-cantilever, and thus leaving the floor clear for sweeping. The outlet should be brass-grated and have a 1-inch trap and 2-inch waste-pipe through wall discharging over a grease gulley, which has a catch grit and galvanized iron lifter. It should be unnecessary to add that this gulley must be cleared frequently to prevent any grease or sand flowing into the drains and thus clog them. It is not only desirable to see that all fittings are properly provided with traps, but also to see that they have ventilation-pipes—short pipes connected to top of outlet of trap and carried through to external wall. This will prevent any syphonage of trap, and should not be in any case omitted. Any fittings, however inexpensive, must be fitted up properly. It will not always be possible to have a hot water supply, but there is no reason why it should not be added, and it will certainly greatly improve the comfort of the cottage owner. The expense of fitting is not great. The system adopted should be the cylinder, this being the safest and not liable to explosion in frosty weather. The cylinder is fitted near the kitchen or scullery boiler with a flow or return pipe from boiler to same. It has a cold service-pipe brought from the cold-water tank somewhere in the roof, with the inlet at the bottom of cylinder which is provided with stop valve. The draw-off taps are all taken from pipe off the top of cylinder; and is carried up to top of cottage, and either taken through roof or turned over cold water tank. The cylinder therefore cannot be emptied and consequently no explosion can take place owing to the water entering at bottom and the draw-off at the top.

VIEW OF COTTAGE AT CHISELHURST

E. J. May, Architect

Chapter VI.—*Materials*

MODERN methods of walling in uniform brick or neatly coursed stone have practically superseded the varied walling of old cottage work, though it is not uncommon to see the old and new styles of building side by side in the same village—so entirely have we lost that sympathetic instinct which led the old builders unconsciously to preserve unity and harmony between one cottage and its neighbour, however unlike the purposes to which they might be put. Variety in walling has gradually come to signify little more than the difference between the laying of stone and of brick. The tendency of modern building is to curtail as far as possible the many legitimate ways of doing things, which the old builders delighted to exercise and multiply, and to reduce them all, as it were, to a common denominator, establishing one that shall be rapid and sufficient, and one to which familiarity has brought a certain dexterous skill. Put an ordinary bricklayer to build a wall of flint and stone, and he will naturally be all at sea. But an intelligent workman with sound local traditions behind him will readily adapt himself to various methods under the guidance of a sympathetic architect to whom these traditions are valuable and inspiring, and who has no wish to uproot them from their soil. The careful choice of a particular stone or brick, the varying in depth of the courses in some interesting way, the use of flint with brick, of stone with flint, of stone with brick, of flint, stone, and brick together, of rough-cast and plaster, of brick with half-timber, and of weather tiling or boarding—all these are legitimate methods of walling open to the English cottage-builder. Cob walls again afford a further variety; but neither this nor any of the other methods must be adopted at random. Knowledge and discrimination must be brought to bear upon the choice. The cob walls and thatched roofs of Devonshire would be quite out of keeping in the north. Surrey has its own brick walls and tile-hung gables; Sussex its thatch, brick, and weather-boarding; Wiltshire its stone and flint; Hampshire its brick and flint; Yorkshire its brick and stone; and Lancashire its stone. East Anglia again has flint and stone. In Wiltshire we find flint panels alternating with stone; the latter occupying more space on the bed than the width of the flint. By this arrangement the ends of the stones overlap one another, building the flint together. This is a procedure that can be varied considerably without getting too far out of bounds and losing the character of the method. Another kind of combination of flint and brick is quite as distinctive in its way—it consists of

50

INGLE IN PARLOR.   A COTTAGE AT CHISELHURST
E. J. May, Architect

strengthening a flint wall by horizontal bands of brick two or three courses deep about every 2½ feet in the height of the cottage, and vertical uprights, also of brick, placed a little

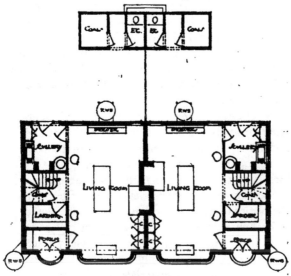

Ground Floor

A PAIR OF WEEK-END COTTAGES, SUSSEX

G. Ll. Morris, Architect

farther apart. These latter are "toothed"— that is to say, uprights of 18 inches in length are alternated with others 14 inches long. This method is common in Hampshire, and a variation of it occurs in Wilts. Other counties have their own peculiar methods, each giving ample scope for simple variations in detail, and the more imaginative and open-minded of modern architects have been quick to find this out. The cottages of Mr Guy Dawber are charming examples of what to build in Gloucestershire. He has caught the spirit of the old Gloucestershire cottage without falling into the mistake of merely trying to get an "old" effect, and his knowledge of local traditional forms subserves his individual way of treating them.

For notwithstanding a good deal of purely sentimental idealisation that is lavished on old cottages because they are old, it remains a fact that a large measure of the beauty of ancient buildings is that which is bestowed upon them by the hand of time. In other words, one of the vital secrets of building is the choice of materials which shall not deteriorate but be enhanced in appearance by the wear and tear of life. Age, if it does not generously transfigure what it touches, only serves to make the ugly uglier, and some materials seem to need its influence to give them any beauty at all. It is not sufficient that the stuff of which a home is built shall just survive the passing of the years; it must respond to them with that mysterious sympathy which the master-hand quickens even in inanimate things. This is a point which the old builders understood unconsciously, and we need not here dilate upon the charm of time-worn brick and timber, the mellow tints of metals, or moss-covered stones, in order to show how admirably such materials were chosen for the durability of beauty as well as the durability of wear. Lead and iron rightly treated, certain kinds of stone, and the best clay-products have this power of "growing old gracefully" in a high degree, but

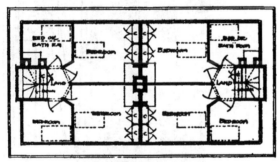

First Floor

A PAIR OF WEEK-END COTTAGES, SUSSEX
G. Ll. Morris, Architect

such poor concoctions as stucco, for example, have none of it; they are irredeemable, and should be banished for ever from "desirable building sites."

In Kent and Sussex, stone cottages are often finished with brick, and these are sometimes—but not always—of later date. Their main characteristics are their simplicity of form, and the way they seem always seeking to maintain an unbroken line. In Yorkshire and in Northamptonshire

A Pair of WEEK END COTTAGES

G.LL.MORRIS Ltd.

40 THEOBALDS ROAD, W.C.

stone cottages are the rule, and in the latter
county the rich yellow-ochre colour of the stone

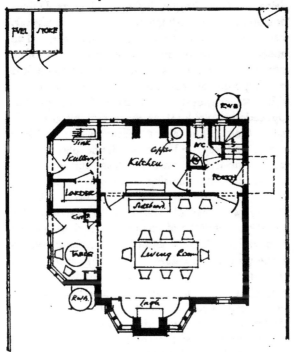

Ground Floor

SHOWING PLAN OF LIVING ROOM IN A WEEK-END COTTAGE
(Three Bedrooms and Bathroom on First Floor)
Designed for Messrs Smee & Cobay by G. Ll. Morris, Architect

is highly characteristic, and gives its distinct keynote to the somewhat flat but verdant and pastoral

landscape. As we move eastward, over marsh and fen countries, and among the broads and plains of East Anglia, lighter and more Dutch-looking methods, with much lime-wash and plaster, seem perfectly to suit the spirit of the place. The modern method of rough-cast walling is often convenient here, and supplies a pleasant and less exacting medium than those discussed above. It is in fact the best of all methods for general application when local or more difficult materials fail. One might almost paraphrase a familiar maxim and say, "When in doubt play rough-cast,"—for it is at once the least and most local of materials, harmonising equally well with tiles, stone, brick, thatch, and slate. Mr C. F. A. Voysey was one of the first to discover this useful characteristic of rough-cast, and to employ it in various districts without any artistic offence to the peculiar "localness" of neighbouring work. In some methods the gravel is pressed into the matrix by hand and worked in patterns. Simple effects may also be obtained by scratching the plaster with some decorative device.

The question of the thickness of the walls is important in relation to climate and materials. Walls should increase in thickness, not in proportion to the cold, but in proportion to the wet. A rainy country needs walls of double courses with a hollow space between. In Surrey and Sussex no amount of weather-boarding—freely though it

VIEW OF INTERIOR OF THE SAME WEEK-END COTTAGE

For Messrs Smee & Cobay

is used for that purpose—is really enough to keep a house dry. Anyone about to build in this or any district exposed to driving rains should adopt these hollow walls. In Sussex, for instance, it has been found advisable to build the walls in two 9-inch thicknesses with the space between filled in with cement concrete, or in those cases where tiling, weather-boarding, or rough-cast is used, one 9-inch and one 4½-inch thickness with space as before will be sufficient, but under no circumstances will a wise architect undertake to erect a house in such neighbourhoods without making sure the walls will be weather-proof. In some places it has been shown that the fierce rains will get through a 14-inch or even 18-inch ordinary brick wall. At the same time in bleak and exposed places as much depends upon sound construction and good finishing as upon actual thickness of walls. The principle to be borne in mind—as we shall note again when we come to consider ventilation—is not only to keep out the cold, but to admit fresh air and sun. In districts sheltered enough to admit of the walls being fairly thin, they may be both strengthened and beautified by the addition of suitable buttresses. These, when made a vital part of the structure, give by their straightforward serviceableness a decorative effect. It is only when added as ornament, and not essential to the wall, that they become a vicious affectation, like boards laid upon a frontage to imitate half-timber, or the foolish stucco battlements that mock some mild suburban residence with the pretence of a fortress and guns.

The use of weather-boarding and weather tiling, so pleasantly common in the south of England, affords another variety in the treatment of the upper storey of a cottage or house. Weather-boarding, indeed, may often be employed to cover the whole of the exterior walls, and can then consist, in sheltered places, of any light and inexpensive frame-work,—given a good foundation of brick or stone up to the floor or sill level. The wood, if deal, can be tarred or painted; if elm, it mellows and improves greatly by wear. But against such use of weather-boarding prohibitive bye-laws are very apt to step in, and thus a decorative and convenient method of work is practically lost to the modern world. Weather-tiling, however, is in all old work confined to the upper storey, partly perhaps because it is felt to belong properly to roofing, and to be in fact only a matter of bringing the roof-covering down upon the main body of the building, and partly also because on the lower levels the tiles might get knocked and broken. A great deal of variety may be obtained in the laying of weather-tiling, but it is better, in view of the general harmony and coherence, to avoid those fanciful arrangements from which even the old tiling is not altogether free. Very pleasing effects are to be had with plain tiling, introducing two or three rows of fancy tiles in the gables, or some of lozenge shape, or with some slight variation in colour. It is always necessary, however, that where the hanging finishes two or three courses of plain tiles should

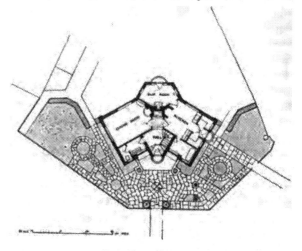

Ground Floor

CHILDREN'S COUNTRY HOLIDAY COTTAGE, SURREY
Cecil Brewer & A. Dunbar Smith, Architects

be used. Care should be taken to avoid tiles having that hard and metallic appearance which neither age nor custom can make pleasant to the eye. The gauge in tiling should be from 3½ to 4 inches,—never more than the latter; and when possible the tiles should be slightly curved. No

one who is familiar with old German methods, as
they may still be seen for instance in such towns
as Heidelberg, can forget the wonderful charm of
the tiling on upper storeys and around dormer
windows, where materials apparently hard and

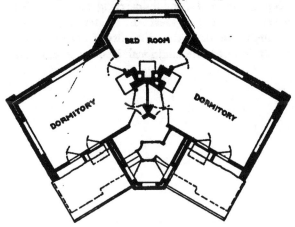

First Floor

CHILDREN'S COUNTRY HOLIDAY COTTAGE, SURREY
Cecil Brewer & A. Dunbar Smith, Architects

unyielding have become so plastic under the
artist's hand, and allowed themselves to be so
cunningly tucked and folded round the awkward
corners, that the very touch of the dexterous
fingers seems to dwell upon them still.   Without
plagiarising this delightful method of tiling and
slating, modern architects should note that in our

61

own country a similar but more simple means has been adopted occasionally. Instead of the roofs mitreing in a hard line the tiles or stone slates have been worked round the valley; this it need hardly be said is rather an expensive way of connecting two roofs, and in carrying out, it needs a great deal of care lest the water should get through, but once this difficulty is overcome, the result is worth the additional labour and expense.

CHAPTER VII. — *Planning of Rooms*

THE necessary dependence of the inside accommodation of a house upon the shape of the outside seems obvious enough as soon as we think about it. Yet it is surprising to find how many people forget it when they begin to discuss the arrangement of their rooms. They fail to realise that if the exterior is to be square and compact, the rooms within cannot be all curves and corners, with winding passages, and nooks in unexpected places, neither can they break forth into bay windows if the exterior elevation is to be kept flat, unless the bay is planned in the thickness of the wall. On the other hand a house of a fanciful form and pattern cannot be divided up into neat rooms of equal size into which all our old carpets and furniture will comfortably fit. The picturesque exterior may involve practical difficulties to the despair of the housewife within. If we want the warmth and beauty of a steep-pitched roof, we must not expect the top rooms to have flat ceilings. In cottage-building, as in most of our worldly enterprises, we find that "we cannot eat our cake and have it," and we must be prepared at many points to sacrifice ideal

63

beauty for practical comfort, and to do without a great convenience in order to get a greater.

The first question, therefore, to be considered in the planning is: What rooms are the most important to the family that is to live here? Are we to provide for family life in the sense of constant companionship and leisure, or is the planning to be done primarily from the point of view of work? Are the members of the household in the habit of spending most of their time together in common pursuits, or will they want, for reasons of occupation or of temperament, to live a good deal apart? Shall we provide what are practically separate living-rooms for the student and breadwinner who will only join the general circle in the evening and at meals? Or do we want a comfortable general room in which to spend most of the day, with bedrooms to which we only go to change our clothes and to sleep?

To meet this last contingency many modern architects are strongly urging what is called the main living-room plan, which provides one large and airy apartment in which all dwell together, and all the ordinary work of the house, except quite dirty work, such as boot-cleaning, is done, the central hall and separate staircase are abolished, and the remainder of the building consists of bedrooms upstairs and a scullery with its surrounding offices below. Messrs Raymond Unwin and Barry Parker, in their handbook,

64

"The Art of Building a Home," have specially favoured this method of room-arrangement. Undoubtedly it has great advantages in the way of domestic economy and hygiene. It saves space and labour, and the multiplication of heating and lighting centres, and it is obviously more healthy to spend one's time in a large room in which the chief heat of the house is conserved than to pass to and fro among rooms of very different temperatures, connected by landings and passages which are permanently cold. In the plan under consideration, the stairs ascend from the main living-room and share its warmth, and the entrance from the street is only screened off by a small porch, or double doors, sufficient to keep the direct draught from the occupants.

The obvious objection to this arrangement is that it does away with all privacy in domestic life. It is admirably suited to married couples, or small and mutually devoted families who like to spend all their time together when indoors. But for the unhappy individual who wants sometimes to sulk, to read and write in silence, or to exchange confidences with an intimate friend, there is no alternative between the street and his bedroom. Perhaps, however, the plan finds more favour with old people than with anybody else, especially if a roomy and cosy inglenook is provided for them. Generally, if they come downstairs and are present at meals, they like a permanent coign of vantage where they may watch the life of the household and feel themselves at one with its interests and cares, catch a glimpse of callers, and hear the news of the day. Unless they are quite invalids and crave for seclusion, it is both dull

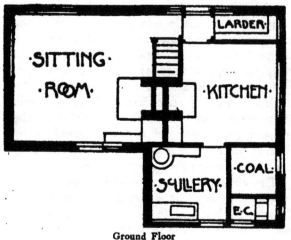

Ground Floor

COTTAGE AT CLANDON
Harold Falkner, Architect

and demoralising for them to be shut away in a separate room and visited periodically by one or another, like a person living in a different world. On the other hand, if a bedridden relative or permanent invalid is to be provided for (and for such people a sunny and pleasant outlook is of the greatest value) it will be very desirable to have their apartment on the ground floor, unless this should prove too noisy for their peace. In such a case we discover the value of a single room at the end of a passage, or placed at some angle where the rooms that flank it shall be quiet. This

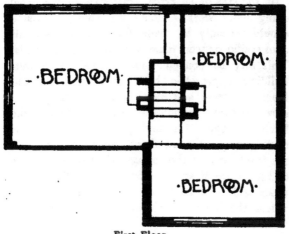

First Floor

COTTAGE AT CLANDON
Harold Falkner, Architect

advantage is afforded by an L-shaped house, or any in which some separate wing stands out from the rest; and the L may very properly be divided into the noisy end and the quiet one. For we must not forget that the people who want to make a noise, such as children, gossips, and manual workers, have just as much right to their noise as the students and invalids have to their quietude; and it is no easy matter for an active person to maintain an unnatural stillness and silence because of somebody resting or writing in the next room.

In the case of an artist, craftsman, or mechanic doing daily work at his own home, provision should certainly be made for him to have his own studio or workroom separate and inviolable. This may be conveniently arranged as an out-building, approached both from the house and from the street, and may often be warmed by a stove backing upon the wall containing the kitchen range. Or perhaps if the worker is dealing frequently and directly with his customers, the front room of the cottage will have to partake of the nature of an office or shop, and the living-room will have to be curtailed in consequence, unless the house is double-fronted, and allows them to be of similar size, with a passage or stairs between. A more economical arrangement is a small lobby, just enough for brief parlance and the accommodation of umbrellas, immediately within the front door, and having an inner door on each side of it—one opening into the work-room and the other into the living-room or house. The stairs may then ascend from the living-room, and beyond them another door lead out into the back-kitchen or scullery. The place of the stairs is, indeed, very often the crux of cottage building;

VIEW OF COTTAGE AT CLANDON
Horace Falkner, Architect

A COTTAGE WITH STABLES
W. H. Cowleshaw, Architect

for a really comfortable flight, with broad steps and not steep, takes up more room than can well be afforded, unless they form part of an inhabited room. One very good method, when it is not desired to bring the stairs into the living-room, is to set them in a compact hall, into which the front door opens, and which has a fireplace of its own. A fire here will warm the main gangway of the house in winter, and with a couple of chairs this little hall may serve as a handy reception room for callers who only come on business or for a brief chat, and whom for any reason we do not care to bring, as it were, into the bosom of the family. The problem of what to do with the casual caller is often a very real one, and of constant recurrence, in small houses where the formal drawing-room has been abolished. One does not like to keep him standing on the front door mat; one does not want him in the living-room when the children are being bathed, and even if there is another room unoccupied, one cannot afford to keep a fire there continually on the mere chance of someone coming in. In cases where callers are frequent and apt to be intrusive, it is a great convenience to be able to receive them in some place where, without seeming actually inhospitable, one does not feel bound to ask them to stay. The hall with comfortable seats and a fire, as above suggested, is a benefit to the whole house, and makes a great difference to the comfort of going to and fro in it. When there are no children, and the domestic life is leisurely and simple, the main living-room may perhaps be accessible to callers at all hours, but it is not everyone who will be found willing to make it so.

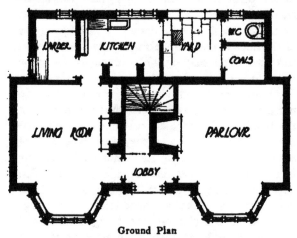

Ground Plan

COTTAGE AT CHISLEHURST, SURREY

R. F. Atkinson, Architect

The difficulty arises in another form when a family having sufficient mutual interests to enjoy a common living-room, yet have by no means the same circle of friends. A caller comes to see one member of the household, and there is perhaps no habitable room where ten minutes' privacy can be had. This difficulty is felt equally by the older

members of a family and the young; for while
the former will naturally have friends coming to
them with troubles not meant for the children's
ears, it is no less to be supposed that young
people just growing up will have visitors whose

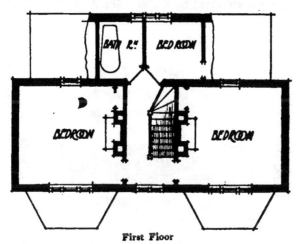

First Floor

COTTAGE AT CHISLEHURST, SURREY

R. F. Atkinson, Architect

confidences should be respected, and to whom the
opportunities for a *tête-à-tête* indoors should, if
possible, be ungrudgingly given. In some of
Mr Voysey's plans there is an excellent provision
made for a small smoking-room or lounge, leading
out of the main living-room and so arranged as to
get some of its heat, where several persons may

71

be comfortably harboured for a brief chat, or while meals are being laid or cleared.

One of the strongest arguments for the main living-room plan is that it does away with the wasteful " best room " in which so much valuable space is sacrificed by the household for five or six

COTTAGE RESIDENCE CHISLEHURST : J. RAE MILTON A.R.I.B.A. ARCHT.

days out of seven, and given over to the keeping of " best " things which have to be regularly dusted, and among which nobody ever feels comfortable or at home. The abolition of such a room will no doubt help immensely towards the simplification of life and the adoption of the golden rule, to have nothing in the home which we do not know to be useful or think to be beautiful; but the transition period presents problems of its

own. What, for instance, is to be done with the
sky-blue silk cushion which Aunt Mary gave us
at Christmas, and which she will most certainly
expect to see upon the sofa when she calls? If
kept in a living-room it may perhaps be made to
wear a simple print cover which can be quickly
whipped off when she knocks at the door, but the
chief objects of abolishing the "best room" are
that people shall take us as they find us, that we
shall hoard nothing too fine for our daily surroundings, and that we shall spare ourselves the
undignified scramble which too often occurs in a
household as soon as footsteps are heard at the
gate. On points like these depend the decision
as to what rooms are essential to our particular
cottage plan.

We have said so much for the abolition of the
"best room" that there is a danger lest this zeal
for household reform tempts us to be impatient
with those who still cling to the old traditions.
Whatever we personally feel, there is no question
that to many people the "best room" is in a real
sense the "holy of holies": the sanctuary of the
home. Within its four-and-a-half brick walls
are mementos closely connected with the life of
the family: here, over the door, is a certificate
showing the progress of son or daughter: there,
in the place of honour, a tea-service given for
years of work in some good cause. Crowding
the room are symbols of success and failure, and

objects round which have gathered both pleasant and melancholy associations. As a "practical" man we shall probably despise this mixed collection of sentimental memories, but in the transition from one way of living to another we cannot

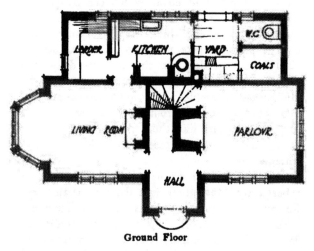

Ground Floor

A COTTAGE IN STAFFORDSHIRE
R. F. Atkinson, Architect

afford to ride rough-shod over these traditions of the front room.

We may indeed, in a remorseless and reforming spirit, delete the room from our plans for the workman's dwelling, because it is best for him, but he will surely find a place, whether it be the bathroom or a cupboard, for these objects of interest. In a broad sense, then, the best room is the private chapel, and stands in somewhat the same relation to the house and home life as Westminster Abbey and its monuments do to the nation.

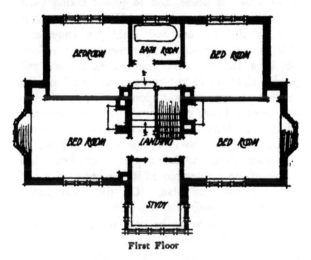

First Floor

A COTTAGE IN STAFFORDSHIRE
R. F Atkinson, Architect

Neither the sacred objects of the home, nor the sacred monuments of Westminster, are particularly beautiful in themselves, but they both symbolise the need in man for a " place apart," an habitation, as it were, for the expression of his most intimate life.

The question of building and furnishing the upstairs rooms as bed-sitting-rooms (if we may use a word so spoilt by its association with cheap lodgings) may be well worth consideration if one or two members of the household are likely to work much at home, and to prefer taking their visitors into their own room. If this is done, it is essential that the bed and washing arrangements shall be properly and neatly screened or curtained off, by means of a solid frame-work or stout rail carried right across the room,—not by a limp and ineffectual drapery hung upon a string attached to odd nails or hooks on the wall. A casual mixture of the appointments of a parlour and a sleeping apartment gives the aspect of a lumber-room of the worst kind, and in no part of the house is a makeshift so intolerable as in the carrying out of a bed-sitting-room plan. On the other hand, when skilfully contrived, the worker's own private living-room may be as healthy, seemly, and comfortable as any in the house; especially if he can avoid the unwholesome and untidy plan of improvising a bed on what is a couch during the day. The real bed (and of course there should be a couch as well if space permits) should be so placed that its curtain or screen may be thrown back at night to allow free ventilation, and to let the occupant of the bed get a good light from the window for early morning reading, as well as his full share of warmth from the fire. A remarkably good example of this treatment of students' bed-rooms has been set by Messrs Smith & Brewer in their design for the collegiate settlement in Tavistock Place, London, where the residents are assumed to have their own private life upstairs, but to give a good deal of their time to the educa-tional and social work of the place, and to share the common rooms for recreations and meals. Here of course the "combined room" plan is carried out on a handsome scale, but there is no reason whatever why it should not be adapted to the modern cottage, and carried out in a straight-forward and unpretentious way.

In plans which spread themselves over an oblong, or the arms of an L or T shape, it is often difficult to avoid wasting valuable space in landings and passages—the alternative being to make some of the rooms open into one another, which is not always a convenient thing. The outermost rooms in such plans—and indeed any wing that stands out from the main body of the house—will naturally tend to be cold in winter; and in cottages having only one storey above the ground floor (which indeed is the general limit of a cottage) this part of the building may well consist, where possible, of the kitchen, with a bathroom over it. Thus all the water arrangements, upstairs and down, may be kept together; and the kitchen stove, hot-water pipes, and tanks connected with it will warm all that quarter of the house.

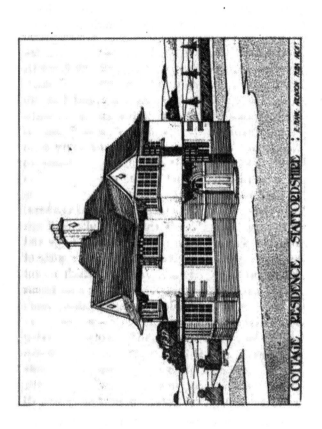

COTTAGE RESIDENCE, STAFFORDSHIRE.

Planning of Rooms

The rooms designed expressly for bedrooms should be no less carefully considered beforehand, as regards shape and wall-space, lighting and ventilation, and the relative positions of the window, fireplace, and door. They ought not to

COTTAGE RESIDENCE CHISLEHURST · GARDEN FRONT · A.B. "27"

be so built that the bed can only stand where the door opens directly upon it, or where, in case of illness or extreme weather, it can get no warmth from the fire. A sitting-room or workroom also should be so disposed that the occupant may have the fire behind or beside him, and the window before. To give small rooms an air of spaciousness requires no little thought and care in putting the fire where it may do most good, deciding which way doors should open, and leaving free as much valuable wall-space and cupboard-room as possible. Attention to little points of this kind will make all the difference between success and failure, and, as we have already hinted, the lesser of two evils will often have to be the final choice. There is always —to put it more hopefully—a better and a worse way of doing things, and the good architect will be careful to choose the better. He will bear in mind, in designing each room, what is its most important feature. Just as the chief factor in the living-room is the fireplace, so that of the bedroom is the bed, and this should always be shown in the plan, in its relation to the window, door, and chimney. Some modern doctors consider it important to place the bed with its head towards the north, believing that in this position the magnetic currents act more favourably upon the body in sleep.

There is a great deal to be said in favour of a separate room as a playroom, both for children and older folk, when the housewife prefers to keep the common room for work, and for the routine and decorum of meals. It serves, in the first place, as a frank acknowledgment of the rights of recreation. It adds considerably to the gaiety of nations for people to know that there is at least one place in the house where they are privileged to make a noise and a mess. An admirable plea for the play-room, under the title "The Best Room in the

A ROW OF COTTAGES AT COLINTON

R. S. Lorimer, Architect

House," * was recently made by Mr Eustace Miles, the well-known tennis champion, in an article deploring the waste of space that occurs in the majority of homes, where the "best room" is an emporium of ornaments and wedding-presents, instead of being a meeting-ground for parents, children, and guests alike, in their freest and happiest hours. "It is not meet," he says, "to take the children's and the parents' room and give it unto callers and furniture."

A great advantage of having the playroom on the ground floor is that it may then be paved with brick. This is sanitary, and easily cleaned after games, in which much dust might be kicked up from boards and carpets, and it lends itself particularly well to the joys of soap-bubbles. These yield delights in which the young-hearted of every age may share. A lady well known in the intellectual world, and the widow of a great mathematician, and herself a grandmother, said the other day, "I hope that as soon as I get too old to blow soap-bubbles I shall die!"

Under some circumstances it may even be convenient to put the kitchen in the attics, especially when the heating and cooking are done by gas, and the heavy labour of carrying coals is avoided. An upstairs kitchen has many advantages if it can be made easy of access without transmitting the sitting-room, if a well-constructed rubbish-shoot

* *C. B. Fry's Magazine* (George Newnes, Ltd.), Sept. 1904.

be built in the outer wall, and if there will generally be some one downstairs to answer the door.
On the other hand, there is sure to be a keen
competition for the attics when the parcelling out
of the various rooms is first discussed. The least
sociable members of the family will want to appropriate them because of the seclusion and independence they afford; and if there be an artist among
us, he will beg to have them for the sake of the
light. But the children will vote for the attics as
a playroom, especially if there be beams in the
roof from which a swing or a giant-stride can be
hung. If not, a swing or horizontal bar, or both,
may easily be contrived in the doorway, and other
simple gymnastic apparatus be arranged in different
parts of the room. The window may be protected
by a movable wire netting from breakages by balls,
and some safe place may be found for a large
mirror, which will be an encouragement and
an aid to self-correction when careful muscular
exercises are being done. Walking, stretching,
balancing, arm and leg movements of all kinds,
and "relaxation" exercises, that can be performed
lying down, may be practised with the aid of an
inclined plank resting at the upper end on some
convenient ledge, or on the window-sill, and
reaching across to the base of the opposite wall.
Given a clear room with plenty of air-space, there
is hardly any limit to the variety of games and
gymnastics, with or without light apparatus, that

may be enjoyed. A playroom wants very little heating, and for this, if upstairs, a small fire-place can generally be arranged against the main chimney stack, especially as all active exercise will be taken with open windows. It is, however, only in nurseries and invalids' sleeping quarters, and rooms where much sedentary work is done, that a coal fire becomes a necessity, or at least very much to be preferred for the sake of the health of the occupants. The playroom, however, will not be without one or two comfortable seats for on-lookers, who may gradually be wooed to take a mild part in game or drill. And when the cult of the body is fully believed in — when physical development is regarded as a part of education and citizenship—perhaps the household will assemble for exercise as regularly as once upon a time it assembled for prayers.

CHAPTER VIII. — *Roofs and Chimneys*

FAMILY life in a cottage naturally tends to focus itself round the main living-room fire. Even in larger and more ceremonious establishments, we all know the charm often exercised by the kitchen fire over the

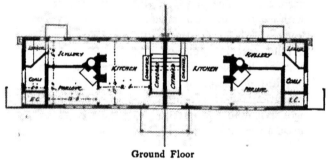

Ground Floor

A PAIR OF COTTAGES, SHOTTER'S MILE
C. F. A. Voysey, Architect

entire household, and how its members love to gather there for confidential chats, rather than round the· dining-room or drawing-room hearth, with its numerous steel fittings, ever reminding us that we dare not eat an orange in its neighbourhood, and can only poke the fire tentatively for fear of making a mess. No patent fuel or special "combustion" grate, no marvel of modern

84

stove-building, however convenient and economical, can for a moment compensate the dweller
in the ingle-nook for his freedom to poke the
fire as he pleases. The familiar saying that we
must know a person seven years before we may
do this in his own house has its basis in the same
proprietary sentiment. A fire which we may not
poke is never truly our own; it is a stranger and
a hireling, and we are never thoroughly at home in
its company.

First Floor

A PAIR OF COTTAGES, SHOTTER'S MILE
C. F. A. Voysey, Architect

The fire-place of the main living-room must,
above all things, then, be inviting, hospitable, and
comfortable to lounge in, sheltered from draughts,
and large enough to accommodate all the household and the occasional "stranger that is within
the gates." Everything possible should be done
to make its fittings simple, convenient, easily
cleaned, and not easily spoilt or tarnished; so
that on festal nights chestnuts and apples may
be roasted, snap-dragon played, and even toffee
cooked without bringing down a rain of chilling

remarks from the house-mother as to how long it will take Betsy to clear up the hearth next day.

In the planning of a room care must be taken to have the fire-place large enough to suit its dimensions, and so well placed as to warm it equally; or at least not to leave any part of it hopelessly out in the cold. Very often it is both convenient and economical to set it across the corner of the room, where the cold "recesses" otherwise formed on each side of it, on a flat wall, will be avoided, and windows may be freely opened without spoiling the comfort of the fireside. For the modern architect plans his windows with a view to their being open while people are sitting round the fire—a thing unheard of in our grandmother's days, when the most approved method of "keeping warm" was to shut the windows, and only open them for "airing" when the room was out of use. To sit with them open beside a blazing fire would then have been considered gross waste of fuel. We seem but lately to have discovered that there is nothing so chilling to the marrow as the peculiar coldness of stagnant atmosphere in a room where fresh air and the heat of a generous hearth are never allowed to play freely together.

In planning any part of a house, it is well to go back again and again to test ourselves with elementary questions as to the why and wherefore of what we are doing. The object of a fire is to

86

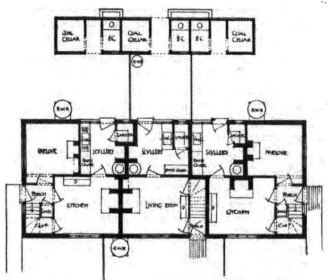

Ground Floor

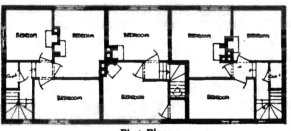

First Floor

THREE COTTAGES, PUTTENDEN, SURREY
F. W. Troup, Architect

warm the room, and if it does not do this effec-
tively, there must be something wrong with its
position, or the stove and its setting. The
object of the hearth is to catch the embers, and
incidentally to reflect heat into the room. Materials that radiate heat instead of absorbing it
should therefore be used as far as possible in
the immediate neighbourhood of the fire. The
object of the mantelpiece and chimney is to protect
the dwelling-house from contact with the flames,
and to convey the smoke safely and directly to its
outlet. And this is to be done with the least
possible waste of heat, and a minimum of dirt
and trouble to the household. The form of the
grate and chimney-piece as seen from the room
may in itself be decorative, and often is so; but
whatever ornament is added to it can only justify
itself by being beautiful, appropriate, and restful
to the eyes, that will perforce be drawn to dwell
upon it, perhaps for many hours together.

In a well-known encyclopedia, a chimney-piece
is pompously described as "the assemblage of
architectural dressings around the open recess
constituting the fire-place in a room." It might
more simply and fitly be spoken of as the decoration link between the fire-place and the room.
Before the fifteenth century, in England the
chimney-piece was merely an enlargement of the
flue over the hearth, forming a hood of masonry
—a real necessity to gather the smoke together

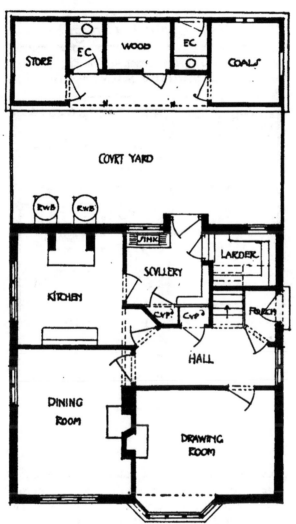

STORE   EC   WOOD   EC   COALS

COURT YARD

RWB   RWB

SINK   LARDER

SCULLERY

KITCHEN

CUP   CUP   PORCH

HALL

DINING ROOM

DRAWING ROOM

A FARM COTTAGE, PUTTENDEN (GROUND FLOOR)
F. W. Troup, Architect

over the fire before it reached the flue proper; from that time onwards it has become more and

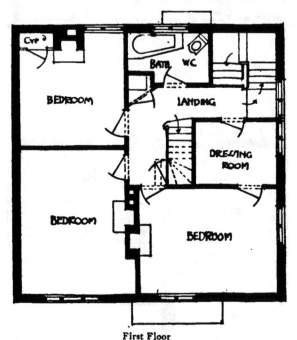

First Floor

A FARM COTTAGE, PUTTENDEN
F. W. Troup, Architect

more decoratively treated, and the stone hood disappeared and has become the modern chimney breast, generally a 9-inch or 14-inch projection from the wall. The fire-place with a large stone hood, dates back as far as the twelfth century, and at that time similar hoods or canopies of wood and plaster, projecting over the open fire, were

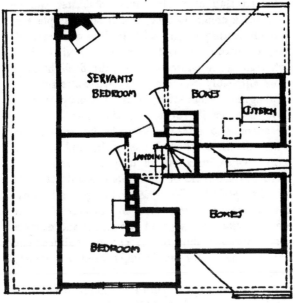

Attic Floor

A FARM COTTAGE, PUTTENDEN

F. W. Troup, Architect

also in use, and probably older than the stone ones.

In a large living-room or hall, a chimney-piece of stone or marble has a dignity and suitability to its place; but in a small apartment such cold and heavy substances are apt to be oppressive in the mass. Now and then a beautiful and richly coloured slab of marble or of alabaster can be used for a chimney-piece, which shall be pleasant and interesting to live with at close quarters. It may be warmly veined with red, or yield those soft translucent whites in which the firelight plays more agreeably than in a hard dead-white streaked with grey. Moreover, most ordinary marbles have been spoilt for us for the time being by the abominations of early Victorian house-building, when the ill-considered use of it, and the still more foolish imitations of it in paint and paper, were characteristic of the pretentious domesticity of the period. We need to get all these barbarisms clean swept from our memories before we can take a fair view of the stones and marbles commonly accessible to the cottage builder, and decide which may be fittingly used in homely dwellings.

Mahogany is apt to afford a similar stumbling-block to some minds. Yet the alternative to stone and marble for a chimney-piece is generally one of the heavier kinds of wood; and the remembrance, the artistic violence done to these materials, in the name of carving or moulding a hundred years ago, often makes us shrink from employing them in a similar way. Happily the modern craftsman is learning that it is possible

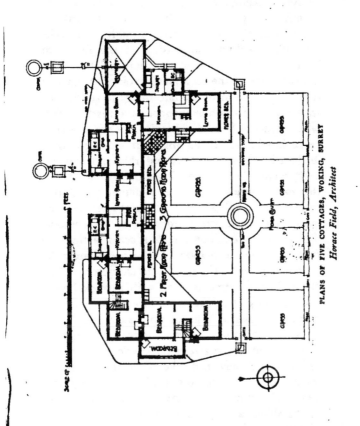

PLANS OF FIVE COTTAGES, WOKING, SURREY

Horace Field, Architect

to treat mahogany in a simple, restrained, and dignified way. The gain, from the æsthetic standpoint, of using a firm, durable, and well-seasoned wood for the setting of the fire-place is that it brings this at once into relation with the furniture of the room, and avoids introducing too many fresh materials into the general scheme; thus making for a homogeneous and restful effect where space is limited. Besides the use of wood, there is still left to us abundant scope for taste in the use of brick. Adopting this, and making, as it were, the chimney itself open frankly into the room without adding superfluous "architectural dressings," we are following perhaps the most simple and straightforward of all methods. The essential condition for its success is that the furniture and decoration of the room must be simple and even primitive in its character. Plain oak and linen harmonise well with a brick hearth and chimney, but the latter are at once felt to be incongruous with much upholstery and highly polished furniture. Glazed bricks and tiles form a convenient link between the crude brick of the ordinary chimney and the decorative ceramics which often frame the modern drawing-room fire. The simplest and least pretentious methods of finishing a brick surface are nearly always pleasing; and in a room soberly furnished with oak and linen the nearest approach to the old-fashioned open hearth—even to the hooks to hang

VIEW OF FIVE COTTAGES, WOKING

Horace Field, Architect

kettles over the fire—will probably be the most satisfactory. Such a hearth should generally have safeguards in the way of a curb or fender. This may sometimes be broad enough to form a comfortable seat for chilly persons and the makers of toast. But such a seat needs to be kept smooth and clean. Padded upholsteries, tapestries, and fixed cushions should never be allowed in the chimney corner, for they harbour soot, coal-dust, and ashes to an extent almost inconceivable to those who have never known the labour of clearing the dust from them from day to day. All mats, rugs, and chair or sofa pillows for a cottage, should be loose, light, and easily shaken.

Of the materials used in framing the fire, marble and stone will generally be found too expensive in the ordinary way, and certainly not so suitable as wood for this purpose in a country cottage. The same objection can be urged against the use of metals like brass, steel, or copper, and amongst woods mahogany will be found costly. The use of oak and pine, painted white or some pleasant colour, will usually be the materials within the scope of the builder of a small cottage. Brick and a judicious use of ordinary plain tiles, as already mentioned, can also be used with good results. It is of importance that when the brick or tile work shows, it should be carefully done, and no attempt made to obtain "artistic" effects with bad workmanship. We have known architects who seem to imagine inferior bricks, badly built, with sloppy jointing, in some mysterious way yield artistic results. It is absurd also to suppose that there is some especial merit and beauty in leaving the roof timbers showing and the joists naked of plaster; there are occasions where the adoption of such primitive methods are pleasant, attractive, and reasonable, but it becomes ridiculous and an affectation, if used on every occasion without any good reason for so doing.

But when we forsake the open hearth for the enclosed chimney of most modern apartments we are met at once by innumerable rivals in the way of patent stoves and grates, which promise to economise our coal, to consume their own smoke, not to let the fire out, to be self-regulating, self-cleansing, and so forth, ever dazzling the weary housekeeper with dreams of that Utopia in which there is no more dirty work to do. In some of these schemes a patent stove may be easily fixed in an ordinary fire-place, but in others a good deal of reconstruction is required, unless such stoves are provided for in the original plan.

FIVE COTTAGES, WOKING. VIEW SHEWING LAUNDRY

Horace Field, Architect

CHAPTER IX.—*The Hearth*

WE have said that the fireside forms the natural centre or focussing point of family life within doors, or, to change the metaphor, the pivot on which all the domestic arrangements turn. Architecturally,

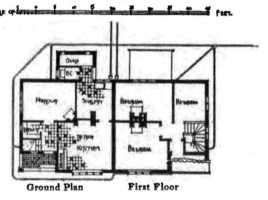

Ground Plan   First Floor

TWO COTTAGES, RIPLEY, SURREY
Horace Field, Architect

therefore, the main chimney is the centre of the house—not necessarily and literally to stand in the middle of it, as in early times, but to bear that vital relation to it that the fire-place bears to the room, so that the other parts are considered and treated in relation to it, and its relative position is always kept in view. The importance of this

G   97

relationship is sometimes better realised from the outside than from within. The chimney is often the first thing seen of a cottage as we approach it from among trees or across the brow of a hill; and it should strike, as it were, the keynote of the building, harmonising with the other exterior features and with the general style.

In the eyes of the poet, the artist, the traveller, the cottage chimney stands as the symbol of human charity, hospitality, and cheer. How welcome to the wanderer, as the day closes in, is the mute and kindly signal described by Wordsworth—

> " Wreaths of smoke
> Sent up in silence from among the trees "—

even if it be not home, but a temporary resting-place, suggesting at least the primitive courtesies, warmth, shelter, and fireside chat! And when more critically considered, from the æsthetic point of view, how important is our first impression of the homestead, gathered from its roof and chimneys! "Take care of the roof, and the house will take care of itself," might become an axiom with architects, and it applies to cottages with peculiar force. In proportion to their size cottage roofs afford the greatest possible scope for variety in materials and arrangement, in coverings and finishings, and in the general plan of the attics, chimney-shafts, and dormer windows.

A chimney, being so homely and practical a

VIEW OF TWO COTTAGES, RIPLEY, SURREY

Horace Field, Architect

thing, should always be simple and unpretentious in character. There is no reason why it should not be ornamented, but it should never be in itself an ornament or appendage instead of an integral part of the scheme. It must never look like something stuck on the top for effect, but always appear to be brought up, as it really is, from the foundations.

Sometimes, in the adaptation of old cottages to modern needs, chimneys have been added to rooms which had none, and these rooms themselves have been cut off from larger apartments by fresh partition walls. It is not easy to make such alterations fit in pleasantly with the original scheme; still less to find any part of the roof in which the addition of a new chimney will not look an intrusion. Fire-places in bedrooms are quite a modern innovation. They symbolise, in fact, the breaking up of the old feudal system on its domestic side, and the growth of individualism, of personal independence — in a word, of privacy for the unit in family life; the antithesis of conditions in the old-fashioned homestead, where the members of the family can hardly get away from each other at all. Undoubtedly the scattering of the household into different parts of the dwelling has had its unfavourable side. The gradual separation of interests between kitchen and parlour, and the banishment of the children to the nursery or attics, has not been always for the better. But it was a necessary stage in the process of civilisation, and architecture must follow it, compromising frankly with the mediæval plan in which everything was grouped round the central hall or living-room, and this alone had a chimney. Whether in the adaptation of an old cottage or the building of a new one, the main chimney should have the dominant place, and any others that may be necessary should be set frankly and unpretentiously, just where they are wanted, trusting to the saving grace of utility to justify them æsthetically, as it generally will.

One of the most characteristic features of old English cottage-building, especially in Surrey and Sussex, is the large exterior chimney flanking one side of the house. This plan is certainly not the most economical for warming the dwelling; but in the days when it was so widely adopted, fuel was much cheaper and more accessible than now, and the labour of carrying it was little thought of. In the densely wooded districts of the south, such as Sussex — where the forests that covered the entire weald were only destroyed in the course of centuries by furnaces for smelting iron ore—one only had to go to one's back door for wood enough to roast the proverbial ox, and the Yule log was never out of season. Only in a country whose resources in the way of timber seemed unlimited could we find such lavish use of it for the framing of cottage walls. It is in the north-west counties, more particularly, that we find the most splendid examples of timbered houses, often with projecting upper storeys, richly set out with curved braces, solid cross-beams, and panels

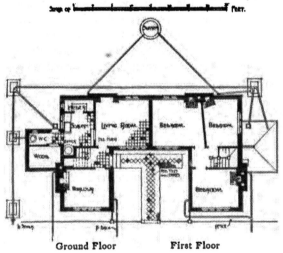

Ground Floor   First Floor

TWO COTTAGES, BRAMLEY, SURREY
Horace Field, Architect

with elaborate diapering and cusping, brought to its perfection. in early Tudor work.

The chief essential of the exterior chimney is that it shall be an integral part of the dwelling, and not appear, as it were, to be slapped alongside as an afterthought, or worse still, have a disconnected look, like a factory chimney, and not

blending obviously and happily with its setting.
Very often this difficulty may be got over by a
small span roof connecting the main roof with
the upper part of the chimney shaft. This also
gives a pleasant break to the roof-line and additional height to the attics, and sometimes allows of
the introduction of a small window in the cheeks.

The general outline of the cottage roof may
either be so treated as to make chimneys, dormer
windows, and deep overhanging eaves the dominant
features, or it may be kept severely simple and
unbroken, and finished by being hipped or gabled
at the ends. The practical advantage of the
steep-pitched roof, with its broad reposeful out-
lines, is that with its ample spaces to accumulate
warmed air it adds considerably to the heat and
cosiness of the house in cold climates and seasons,
besides adding immensely to its appearance. Mr
Ralph Nevill, in his book on Surrey cottages,
says that the pitch of a roof is generally a sure
index of its date; those sloping as much as
60 degrees being earlier than the Elizabethan
period. He also points out how ingeniously
hipped roofs are contrived in the old cottages,
the sharp point being avoided by a small gablet.
No ridge-board was used, but each pair of rafters
pinned together at the top. It was therefore
obviously inconvenient to run the hip-rafters
together to a point, and they were therefore run
each to about 9 inches below the junction of the

pair of rafters. The same thing will be found invariably done with haystacks, the difficulty of forming the point being thus avoided.

Verges or barge-boards were formerly among the most important parts of the exterior decoration of a cottage. These are decorative wooden boards hung at the gable-ends of roofs, and they may, of course, be carved, pierced, moulded, or otherwise adorned in many fashions. Examples still survive in which the tracery is in a very fine design of Tudor roses ; and the lavish labour bestowed on such decoration is characteristic of fifteenth and sixteenth century work.

What dormers are to be put in the roof must, of course, depend upon circumstances. The modern architect has to study economy much more than his predecessor, who would probably leave his steep-pitched roof as a large dark loft, to be beloved by ghosts and children for many a generation, while the modern man has to utilise all possible cubic space for the nurseries or bedrooms. A sloping ceiling is not without its charm, and with a judicious arrangement of windows, the attics are often the most beautiful rooms in the house. Skylights cannot be said to be picturesque from without or satisfactory from within. They are often convenient, and sometimes desirable, but they should only be adopted when it is impossible to get a small window, or even lunette on a vertical plane, or in the cheeks of the span roof aforesaid. A window is naturally and properly something from which one can look out upon the world, and not merely at the sky, and one of the most common mistakes in building is to set the upper windows too high above the floor of the room, so that one has always to stand up to see out of them. Every window in the house should be able to have a window-seat, if desired, and special pains should be taken about the disposition of attic and dormer windows, since they may often command the best view of the road and surrounding country. These positions should always be at the disposal of invalids and sedentary workers, and their aspects to sun and wind should be well considered. Children do not care about a distant view; they are much more interested in seeing what passes near the window. The introduction of covered leads, high balconies, roof-gardens, etc., hardly comes within the scope of a country cottage, being rather one of the compromises and makeshifts of town life; but the addition of a small balcony to one of the top windows, where practicable, is often a great joy to the possessor.

A country cottage should offer no excuse for the ugly modern habit of so building that the set of the roof is concealed by the walls, and these have the appearance of having been built round the roof instead of supporting it. A parapet belongs to a castle or fortress, not to a dwelling-

FRONT VIEW OF TWO COTTAGES, BRAMLEY, SURREY

Horace Field, Architect

house. The shape of the roof and the manner of its setting should always be clearly seen from the roadway, and one of the greatest sources of charm is sacrificed by any attempt to do away with over-hanging eaves. These give distinction and sharpness to the outline, make a picturesque way for watercourses, give hospitality to birds, and to evergreen or flowering creepers, and throw a beautiful shadow on the walls.

The gradual disuse of thatch, and the decay of thatching as a country craft, is one of the deplorable results of enforcing, indiscriminately in rural districts, bye-laws properly suited to a town. In the face of all that can be said for necessary restrictions as to inflammable materials, in view of the devastation of homesteads and villages by fire in times of drought, there yet remains ample room for isolated cottages on sites where they could be no possible source of such danger to their neighbours, and where the builders and tenants have an obvious right to run the risk of fire, for themselves alone, as the price they are willing to pay for a thatched cottage. As a matter of fact the risks of fire are exceedingly small, as is proved by the great number of examples which survive, of considerable age, in districts where this traditional method has been kept up, as in Kent and Sussex, Devonshire, Dorset, Somerset and Hants; and due provision for the danger can be made by each individual householder.

The shape and colour of the chimney should be considered in relation to the prevailing colour of the whole building, and the materials chosen for the roof and the walls. White chimneys strike a restful note when colour has been freely used below; and red ones contrast pleasantly with a thatched roof, or relieve the sombreness of slates. They also go well with rough-cast and with weather-boarding. Even when the chimneys are not arranged in one group, they ought to have a certain unity of treatment. If economy is to be much studied, the shafts themselves may be low, finished with high chimney-pots; and this plan will have the practical advantage of lessening the tendency to down-draughts, especially if the shafts are high as well, which is certainly the best plan. It is obviously desirable that all possible provision against the nuisance of smoky chimneys shall be made from the beginning, in the planning and construction of the chimney shafts and the kind of stoves used in the fire-place, that the outside appearance will not be spoilt by unsightly remedies in the shape of cowls.

No discussion of the chimney question would be complete without mention of the possibility, in the present day, of building a comfortable house or cottage without any chimneys at all. A photograph of such a house, built recently at Longford, near Sevenoaks, was published in the daily press as an illustration of what might be done to banish the

A BACK VIEW OF TWO COTTAGES, BRAMLEY, SURREY
Horace Field, Architect

THE LODGE, "NORNEY," SHACKLEFORD, SURREY
C. F. A. Voysey, Architect

dirt and labour of fire-places from the dwelling, by heating it throughout with hot air pipes, served by a small stoke-hole in the form of an outhouse, no larger or more unsightly than an ordinary coal-cellar.

CHAPTER X.—*Air and Light*

THE question of ventilation in the dwelling-house is one on which there is the greatest difference of opinion among the inhabitants themselves. Every housewife has her own theory as to what constitutes a draught, and how much fresh air is necessary to health and comfort, and what the temperature of the different rooms should be. Unless she is overruled by some individual of stronger preferences and the power to enforce them, the other members of the family will accept and enjoy her ruling—or submit and suffer—according to their different temperaments and to the amount of tact that may be shown by the housewife in dealing with the wishes of the household.

The two chief difficulties in the way of ventilation are, first, the practical one, of building in such a way that fresh air can flow through every part of the cottage without spoiling the comfort of the "cosy corners" in which one sits to read, write, work, or recreate indoors; and secondly, the far more subtle theoretical difficulty of persuading valetudinarians and old-fashioned people that there is no need for them to be cold because the windows are open. They are only cold because of our deep-rooted national meanness of trying to economise firing by shutting our doors and windows and living in stagnant air. Only those who have been accustomed to camp fires in the open country (and should not everybody know this delight at some time or other ?) can fully realise how much of the enjoyment and exhilaration of warmth is lost in a close room, and how far the degenerate town-dweller has strayed, in his efforts to keep out the cold, from the natural and true methods of keeping his circulation in good order — which is what we really mean by keeping warm. Nothing is so depressing and chilling to the system as air grown stale within four walls. Even when only breathed by one or two people it still needs to be constantly changed as well as warmed. Hence economy of fuel is the very last economy that ought to be practised in a climate like ours.

Another essential condition of warmth is to have a reasonable number of windows, and to have them set, whenever necessary, on two different sides of the room. Paradoxical as it may sound, it is often easier to keep a room warm with many windows than with few ; firstly, because if they are well aspected the result will be, "the more windows, the more sun"; and secondly, it is a great convenience to be able to open and close the different windows according to the direction of the wind. The most ardent "fresh-airist"

will naturally grumble if he has to sit at his desk
for consecutive days in the teeth of a north-
easterly gale, without the alternative of closing
the window in front of him and opening one
which faces east or south. Where this is
impossible, a fanlight over the door, to open on
a pivot into the hall or staircase, may sometimes
be arranged.

Large, full-length windows do undoubtedly
make a room cold, unless in a very sunny aspect
and a sheltered site. French windows should
only be adopted where they are likely to be used
for their natural purpose, namely, to make a
way out to a garden or balcony, for it is to
the lower part of a room that protection from
draughts is most needed. A pious writer once
said he did not believe that anybody could maintain a Christian frame of mind for very long with
cold feet. Everything should be done to make
the floor of a room as comfortable and snug as it
can be made without becoming a dust-trap, and
to that end the windows should be set only just
low enough for the occupants to see out of them
without having to stand up. It should be needless to add that all such windows should be made
to open top and bottom, but unfortunately there
are still examples to be found of upstairs windows
opening at the bottom only, serving only to chill
one's knees and feet, while making the proper
ventilation of the room impossible. More

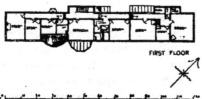

FIRST FLOOR

SCALE

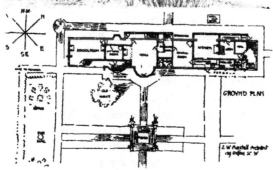

GROUND PLAN

PLANS OF CHERRY CROFT, SUSSEX
E. W. Marshall, Architect

remarkable still, we have recently found a pretty little country house in which the only sitting-room was completely spoilt by windows which opened at the top only, by means of casements placed *above* the long fixed panes, so that in the hottest weather, though the room might be tolerably cooled by having these upper case-ments opened on both sides of it, yet one could never have the pleasure of looking out of an open window in the ordinary way; and a miser-able sense of imprisonment was the consequence.

If the casement system of windows is adopted —and this is undoubtedly the most interesting for a cottage—it is important that the proportion of the windows should not be too long, and if the ground floor rooms are moderately high it will be necessary to introduce a transom for a secondary number of casements, which may be worked by a cord, for use in cold weather, since the undeniable draughtiness of a casement is often made an excuse for keeping it shut. When this plan is adopted, care should be taken to hang the blinds or curtains only as far up as the top of the casement proper, leaving the upper window clear. If, however, this is objected to, and blinds or curtains are demanded to cover the full length of the window space in order to keep out the light, the curtain-rods may be arranged in the soffit of the window, leaving space for a free play of air behind it. If this plan of upper and lower windows is not adopted, the ordinary sash or single casement windows are the most convenient. The essential thing is that every room should have some openings in the upper part by which the air can be changed without letting the wind blow directly on the feet and knees of the occupants. Further, it is a good plan to have at least one ventilator in each room which shall be at the top of the wall ventilating into a chimney stack, otherwise there will always be a layer of stale air just under the ceiling, with very little chance of escape.

The breaking-up of a window into small panes, or "leaded lights," adds very much to the charm of the cottage, and gives the advantage that when one small pane is broken it is easily and cheaply repaired. Plate-glass, except for a mansion, has a hard, commercial look, and is quite out of place in cottage surroundings. The right use of lead with glass for windows and door-panels constitutes one of the most delightful architectural crafts, and in modern days one of the most neglected. Stained glass again affords immense scope for the exercise of taste; a cold and bare-looking passage or staircase may be warmed and brightened by a judicious shaft of coloured light, and in rare cases, where the window space is ample and the aspect good, the introduction of slightly tinted glass may be an improvement to the bedroom or parlour. Blue and green give coolness to an apartment; red increases its apparent warmth. Both red and yellow have a stimulating influence; blue, green, and more especially violet, have a soothing effect on the nerves. The colours, however, must be well chosen and well applied, or they may be too painfully reminiscent of the suburban staircase windows of early Victorian days, which combined so deplorably well with its "grained" yellow-brown painting and the mock-marble paper of its walls.

The framework of casements may be either of wood or stone. The space between the mullions when quarry lead glazing is used may vary considerably, but it is well to keep it within 18 inches at most, and it may, of course, be very much smaller.

The height of the rooms will naturally make a great difference to the appearance of the windows from the exterior as well as to their convenience from within; and indeed it is only when we come to deal with windows that we realise the importance of the rule that, both for comfort and for beauty, no cottage room should be more than 9 feet high unless there is a large hall which takes up the two floors. Several modern architects have made a firm stand for this maximum of height in cottages, notwithstanding many vexatious bye-laws to the contrary, feeling as they do that it is difficult to obtain good

FRONT VIEW OF "CHERRY CROFT"
E. W. Marshall, Architect

proportions in the elevations; instead of being a low structure, it takes on the look of an upstart, and rears itself aggressively, as it must inevitably seem to do when the rooms are loftier than is justified by their horizontal measurement.

Bay-windows, always a pleasant break in a frontage where the general outline is austere, are especially delightful in a country cottage, where one welcomes every fresh opportunity of a sideway glimpse of the distant prospect, and an outpost wherein to watch for comers up and down the road. When "leaded lights" are adopted, nothing can be more agreeable than the plain rectangular form, whether it be for a single window projecting from the ground floor, or overhanging from above, or carried up the whole elevation. The rounded bay so familiar and so decorative in Queen Anne and early Georgian houses seems to need a fairly substantial building behind it, with a very broad and simple outline, and no frittering away of its sober beauty in ornamental detail. The more common wide-angle bays have been somewhat spoilt for us by their association with suburban jerry-building during the last fifty years, but there is no reason why the form should not be pleasing if properly treated and made to harmonise with the general scheme of the frontage. Considered from within, the bay-window, being likely to be a cold place to sit in, should be kept, if possible, within the direct warmth of the fire. In cold and exposed places it may be a great convenience to have a thick curtain, reaching from floor to ceiling, hung straight across the opening of the bay, which may make the room more cosy at night without closing the windows behind it, and may also, when needful, be partially drawn as a draught-screen during the day. The benediction of the housewife from generation to generation will rest upon the builder who provides for fixtures of this sort being easily and firmly attached. At the very least, the topmost three inches of every interior wall beneath the cornice, if there be one, should be absolutely sound for holding strong nails or for fixing a picture rail, from which weights are to be hung, and such woodwork as may hold long screws should be obvious and easily accessible. Curtains on landings and in halls and passages may sometimes be useful, but their disadvantage as dust-traps must never be forgotten. The place in which they must certainly not be put is at the head of any flight of stairs, however small, for here they might easily prove a death-trap to a person unfamiliar with the house, and approaching them from the other side.

Lunettes, or small circular windows—always made to open—are convenient for stairs and landings, and sometimes for rooms also; while for cupboards and pantries they are invaluable. It is to be hoped that the day of the long dark cupboard under the stairs, or in some ill-ventilated corner of the landing, is for ever done. Such cupboards, with their stagnant and stuffy atmosphere, unchanged from one spring clean to another, are the most successful breeding-ground for germs that could well be contrived in any household. Personal clothing, often worn and soiled, is allowed to lie or hang there for months together, either forgotten or regarded as being safely "out of the way." All manner of odds and ends accumulate there, in varying states of dust and dirt, and often of damp also; in short, everything that is not wanted about the house is put into the cupboard, and it requires no little leisure, energy, and moral courage to insist on the regular over-hauling and weeding-out of such accumulations, and the purifying of all dark corners, if possible with light, but certainly with air. However well the house is lit, there will always be some corners, passages, and recesses more or less in darkness, and the important thing to be managed is that these parts of the house should be well aired and ventilated, kept as bare of fixed and heavy furniture as they can be, and only occupied by things constantly in use, so that the contents—and thereby to some extent the surrounding air — get changed in the ordinary course of life. Cupboards facing a door or window are easily kept clean; and when required for stores and things to be taken care of, such as linen and personal belongings, their own doors should be securely shut and no soiled or dusty articles ever put into them. There is a dainty charm about old lavender-scented shelves and clothes-presses where the air is not musty, but kept sweet and fragrant by scrupulous cleanliness of habit and by the sound building and thorough ventilation of the house.

A VIEW FROM GARDEN OF "CHERRY CROFT".

E. W. Marshall, Architect

Chapter XI. — *Fixtures and Fittings*

NOT only is the question of cupboard-room important as regards the proper ventilation of the whole house, but it very largely affects the architectural treatment of the interior, both from the decorative and the utilitarian point of view. The whole interior economy of the house may in fact be enormously improved or deplorably marred by the arrangement of the cupboards. They may be set in unbecoming and awkward places, so that they can never be got at without disturbing somebody and knocking against the back of his chair; or they may be shallow and mean-looking, always tumbling their contents out into the room. No house can long be kept tidy and comfortable in which the cupboard accommodation is inadequate; but the disposal of cupboards and open shelves may make all the difference in the beauty and distinction of the rooms and staircases as well as in the comfort of the occupiers.

The tendency, now clearly marked in many quarters, to build the furniture into the house, is on the whole a good one. It must at least make for stability in domestic life, and simplify the labour of removals, to have not only cupboards and shelves, but also the principal seats and lounges, hat and umbrella stands, and even some of the tables, as permanent fixtures in the dwelling, and not to have to carry heavy wardrobes and cumbersome " suites" from one abode to another. The obvious objection is that it would to some extent prevent the exercise of individuality in house-furnishing; that it would be impossible to please all tastes, and that many would still cling tenaciously to their own furniture, to the last stick, and think no pains too great to preserve it intact through all vicissitudes of change. It is certain, however, that a great number of people would welcome some such arrangement for its convenience and simplicity; just as one accepts certain conventional uniforms such as the cap and apron of maid-servants and the evening dress of men. In one sense they subordinate the personality, but in another they give the best possible scope for its display. It is generally agreed that people who look nice at all look their nicest in some quiet uniform; and similarly no good house-wife would be at a loss for the display of individual taste in her house if the most substantial and universally necessary articles of furniture were provided as a part of the building.

Broadly speaking, the less furniture a room contains the easier it is to keep it clean and habitable. On the other hand a few really convenient and easily opened chests, drawers, and boxes, to hold things in regular but not constant use, will be an immense saving of time, toil, and temper, to say nothing of dusters, brushes, and brooms. The chief nuisance to be avoided is a littered floor. To those who do much work at home, every facility should be given for keeping their tools and materials on a level with their work; neither in various untidy stacks about their feet nor on top shelves, an eyesore to everyone. A workroom completely lined with cupboards may appear an extravagance in a cottage with its limited space; but it is a very real economy if by that means is secured such a clear floor and table space that the room will not take more than a few minutes to sweep and dust every day. The dresser with soundly-built drawers is perhaps the most convenient and dust-proof; cupboards with well-fitting doors come next.

Cupboards above and around the fireplace have the disadvantage of catching all the most objectionable kinds of dust. Books at all events, if their bindings and edges are valued, should be kept the other side of the room. Care should always be taken in the case of upstairs cupboards in the recesses by a fireplace, that there is no leakage into them from the chimney shaft. A lady recently had her prettiest gowns completely spoilt by being hung against a crack in the wall which evidently communicated with the kitchen flue; in fact, in all cases where cupboards are set near the fireplace it is better to keep them for things that are constantly in use, so that they can be frequently dusted and cleaned at least once a week. And the topmost of a series of shelves in a recess, or of a bookcase or dresser, should if possible be hung with well-fitting doors, since the dirtiest air naturally accumulates and drifts about at the top of the room. Curtains running in front of shelves are sometimes convenient if cupboard doors cannot be provided, but they are apt to serve as dust-traps, and need regular brushing and shaking if they are not to make the last state of those bookshelves worse than the first.

A great deal of shelf and cupboard accommodation will depend upon the arrangement of the stairs, and this again will make an enormous difference to the beauty of the interior as a whole. Nothing is more fatal either to comfort or beauty in a cottage than a flight of narrow, straight, and steep stairs, generally with a mean-looking rail at one side—an inhospitable gangway upon which a few human limbs are almost certain to be broken before the house is old. Avoid, if possible, the staircases with a spiral turning half-way; making it a difficult and wasteful job to cover the V-shaped steps with carpet or matting, and often throwing a valuable corner into disuse. A spiral staircase is a picturesque and convenient thing; but when the spiral is merely adopted as a means of getting round the corner it is generally awkward, and

THE LONG CORRIDOR ON FIRST FLOOR, "CHERRY CROFT"
E. W Marshall, Architect

out of keeping with the rest of the stairs. It is nearly always better to treat them in the more natural and straightforward way; making a plain square landing where the turning is required, and then beginning another straight flight, particularly avoiding that odd couple of stairs which many jerry builders love to set in between two flights, or in different parts of the landings and passages, where they are always a danger and a nuisance to persons of short sight and unfamiliar with the dwelling. Still more reprehensible is the custom of putting one step at the door of a room, as has been done in certain modern cottages that we could mention. Only under exceptional difficulties is this necessary, and everything possible should be done to give each floor of the building an unbroken level.

The advantage of broad and shallow stairs is so great, as regards safety and comfort, and the look of simplicity they give to the house, that, if this treatment threatens to take up more cubic space than can well be spared for this purpose, the alternative of throwing the staircase into the main living-room should be seriously considered. If this is done, the incidental cupboard-room, perhaps, will not be quite so abundant, though whether the space immediately under the stairs is to be enclosed will of course be optional. But when a straight staircase runs up the middle of the cottage there will often be space above it for a fine cupboard running between the two main rooms upstairs. Such a cupboard we once knew, whose vaults seemed utterly impenetrable to our childish vision; a treasure-house of which Santa Claus himself must have been the keeper. With a proper distribution of pegs and shelves this may be the most useful storing-place for personal possessions, of which a certain number are only too sure to accumulate, however rigorously one may set oneself in a cottage to lead the simple life. It might easily be argued that cupboards and all such handy receptacles are a dangerous snare, and serve to foster the hoarding instinct so fatal to comfort and cleanliness in a limited space. But we have not all yet risen to the height of that practical philosopher who, when asked by a visitor to his severely bare apartment, "And where do you put your clothes?" was able to answer that he usually put them on.

One kind of cupboard, however, is becoming increasingly popular, necessary, in a modern cottage,—namely, one that can be easily adapted as a photographic "dark room." Of course the main essentials of this are that the door shall be perfectly fitting and that if a window or any other opening occur in it, this can be fully covered with a dark red shutter or screen, removable for ventilation between the acts. The interior fittings must include a seat and a table, or a broad shelf at table-level, and as many smaller shelves as can be accommodated, and if the cupboard is also to be used for general purposes and not given over entirely to the cult of the camera, care must be taken not to leave anything in it (such as hanging garments) that will easily be spoilt by the stains of the developer. Naturally the photographer will prefer, when possible, to do his developing in a bathroom or scullery, for the convenience of running water; but here it is a much more complicated business to shut out all light, and to secure freedom from interruption; as a rule the cupboard makeshift, with all its limitations, is more conducive to domestic peace.

Another much neglected source of beauty among the wood-work fittings is the provision of shutters to the windows, and sometimes to the upper part of doors. In the older cottages, when life was less secure in country districts than to-day, these were important to the safety of the household; but when they were no longer so necessary (thieves finding little to tempt them, and there being generally somebody at home), they became mere ornamental appendages, and degenerated accordingly in form and setting. Now, however, the country cottage is becoming more and more the resort of people with artistic treasures, who like to be able to lock it up securely while they spend a few days in town. The shutter question, therefore, presents itself as a practical one again; and when the old patterns

are modified as they must certainly be to meet
modern standards of ventilation, a new charm may
be added to the windows both within and without ;—for outer shutters in the form of a series of
these louvre boards framed into top and bottom
pieces are pleasant on a wall that gets abundant
sun. They give a decorative note to the exterior,
when thrown back against an otherwise bare
frontage, and afford scope for good colour-
harmonies between the wood-work and the rough-
cast or brick. It is perhaps when they are painted
green, against rough-cast or white plaster, that
these outer shutters look most restful and homely
in their effect, but alternative schemes will readily
present themselves to the designer. For windows
on the ground floor, portable shutters, well fitting
and matching the surrounding wood-work, will
occasionally be convenient, as also for glass-
panelled doors.

INGLE NOOK IN HALL, "CHERRY CROFT"
E. W. Marshall, Architect

M to U

CHAPTER XII.—*Arts and Crafts*

WE may now assume that we have planned our cottage to give the sort of accommodation we require. We have considered its site and the aspects of its different rooms, its drainage and ventilation, its heating and lighting, and some of the main essentials of its furniture. We have provided that the shelter and security of the dwelling are complete, that the materials are suitable and well seasoned, that the doors and windows will easily open and shut, and will not rattle. We will assume further that the materials have been put together with a judicious and a generous hand,—that we have not been building, for instance, for tenants who are likely to chop up the balusters for firewood or deface and destroy light fixtures of a decorative kind. But it is certain that the better the work has been done, the less will there be left to say about decoration. If we have built soundly and simply what we wanted for our practical needs, the chances are that the dwelling will have become beautiful in the making; and in any case we can only here repeat a few of the general principles of decoration, which will really have been in our minds all the time, and should be there from the moment the site is chosen until the cook has put the last touches to the house-warming supper.

We have already spoken of the need of good *proportion* in the exterior, and of the harmonious arrangement and balance of masses, the straightforward use of every device for its natural purpose and so forth—buttresses, for example, not being added as ornaments, but only used to support a thin wall; mouldings, machine carvings and ormolu mountings never being adopted unless they serve a clear purpose in the scheme. It will be well, however, to remind the aspirant that he will not easily find either designers or workmen ready to co-operate with him in making things simple and unadorned, and leaving out superfluous trimmings, nor will he find it cheap to do so. On the contrary, the man who wants a plain cottage will often have to pay more for what is left out than for what is put in. Paradoxical though it may sound, simplicity is the most expensive thing in the market; and the intending builder will seriously deceive himself if, in thinking how little he really wants in the way of a dwelling, he fails to reckon with the dead weight of prejudice and custom which he will have to overcome before he can banish so much as one conventional moulding from his plan. Mr C. F. A. Voysey, who was one of the first modern architects to set his face against these time-honoured tricks of "finish," has told us how he has had to pay again and again for some trivial ornament to be left out of his design because it was so startlingly

unusual, and therefore so highly distasteful, to
the average workman to make, for instance, a
window-sill without a projection, or the jamb of
a door set straight into the wall without any sort
of ornamental flourish. He cannot realise that
"finish" does not necessarily mean ornament or
something emphasised or added, and that a piece
of work may be highly decorative and perfectly
finished without any ornament at all. We
naturally suppose, when we begin to seek these
things, that a perfectly plain door, table, or
bookcase will surely cost less than a "fancy"
one—the word "fancy" having now come to
mean the utter dearth of fancy on the maker's
part and a merely mechanical frothiness of treatment which lets good material run to seed in
ornamental forms that have become sterile by
much repetition, and lost any grace and spontaneity
that they may once have had.

The practical keynote, however, of the costli-
ness of plain fittings lies in the fact that it is
always dearer to have a thing specially made for
us in the way we want it than to accept a standard
pattern which the carpenter, builder, or joiner is
using every day. So long as we are content with
the sort of doors, window-frames, chairs, tables,
balusters and so forth that have become poor in
design and execution as a result of being made by
the dozen or the score, so long will cheap lines
and poor standard patterns be available, but

directly we want a thing simple and with some thought bestowed upon it we shall have to pay the price of its being unique. Hence one of the difficulties *in raising the general standard of design*; for until there is a general demand for good work we must not expect it to be cheaply had.

Next to simplicity of form, the treatment of surfaces claims consideration. This must be suited to the material itself, the general character of the building, and the locality in which it stands. Certain kinds of ornament, quite seemly and beautiful in the remote districts, would look incongruous in a town; while the conventional and perhaps classic styles proper to a city would be out of place in the village or the wilds. Generally speaking, cottage decoration should confine itself to homely and primitive forms. Urns and pilasters do not become it; far more pleasant are the images of favourite birds and common flowers. Metal work for a cottage should be unpretentious in design, in treatment simple and bold. All exterior decoration should be weatherproof, or of a surface that gains in beauty with the marks of many storms upon its face. Wrought iron and lead are of course the most time-honoured materials, the former allowing for a good deal of sharp detail and definition, the latter demanding the opposite kind of treatment—suggestive and sketchy rather than fine. Ornament for such a soft metal as lead should always be modelled and not carved, for it is unsuited to give detail and high relief. The use of lead for pipes and water-tanks is of very ancient history; and in spite of the fact that the modern epidemic of lead-poisoning has cast some doubts upon the safety of the metal even for this universal purpose, it is unlikely that any other so convenient substance will be found to take its place. The probability is that cases of disease supposed to be traced to water-pipes are due rather to accumulations of dust and dirt within them than to the metal of which they are made; but a small scare of this kind may serve a good purpose if it impresses on households the importance of boiling or distilling all such water before using it for the drinking or cooking supply.

Lead holds a unique place among the common metals on account of its smoothness, non-corrosive-ness, and durability. But over and above its serviceable qualities, it has a no less special decorative value which has been too long lost sight of. We are apt to think of lead as the dullest and least inspiring of metals, as far as regards intrinsic beauty or adaptability to artistic ends. We have come to treat it as a sort of Cinderella of the workshop, to be used for dirty and unpleasant purposes, to which we should not think of applying a beautiful stuff. Far otherwise was the spirit of the mediæval craftsman, who thought no human service too menial to be beautifully done. Lead had a much wider range of application at that time perhaps than any other metal; and in its larger architectural uses—in cathedral roofs and spires, and in the walls of palaces—was treated, says M. Viollet-le-Duc, "like colossal goldsmith's work." In that treasure-house of seventeenth-century gossip, the diary of Mr Samuel Pepys, the author describes the leadwork in the palace of Nonsuch, built by Henry VIII. "One great thing," he notes, "is that most of the house is covered, I mean the posts and quarters in the walls, with lead and gilded." Staircase balustrades also were frequently made with panels of pierced and latticed lead, hung between iron standards.

The modern cottage is not likely to afford scope for the revival of leadwork on such an imposing scale, but there is ample room to use it with intelligence and sympathy, both in its strictly utilitarian and in its more decorative capacity. Mr W. R. Lethaby, in his admirable handbook on the subject, describes and illustrates a charming little ventilator found in the wall of an old Surrey cottage, made of a lozenge-shaped piece of pierced lead. Commenting on the neglected possibilities of such work, the author says: "No metal is more perfectly adaptable to noble use through a range of treatments that cannot be matched by any other metal whatsoever. It combines extreme ease of manipulation with practically endless dura-bility, and a suitability to any scale, from a tiny ink well or a medal to the statue of a horse and rider,

THE HALL, CHERRY CROFT
E. W. Marshall, Architect

a Versailles fountain, or the greatest cathedral spire. Only in our century in England would it be possible for the metals which are so specially hers—iron, tin, and lead—to have been so degraded that it is hardly possible to think of them as vehicles of art." There seems no reason why a material so full of traditional charm should not be restored to something of its old dignity, even in the humbler kinds of architecture, and strike again, in course of time, the old and wonderful note of colour which we get in a lead-covered spire or turret, shimmering with its quaint mouldy-blue or green in rain and sun.

It is to be hoped that its decorative possibilities will be recognised more fully by modern builders and architects, and that the old methods of treating pipes, gutter, and rainwater heads will be returned to. In Roman architecture such decorative fittings were so highly thought of that most of the lead work was signed by the plumber.

Pewter and white metal has come very much into use for interior fittings during the last few years, and when used with judgment it is a convenient and effective material for doorplates and handles, small hinges and buttons, and such light decorative finishings as will not receive much strain or hard wear. Locks and keys, bolts and bars, window and shutter fastenings, and the latches and hinges of all large doors

THE GARDEN, "CHERRY CROFT"
E. W. Marshall, Architect

must, of course, be of iron, but there still remains possibilities for white metal fittings where the advantages of a metal that will not tarnish will be keenly appreciated. An enormous saving of labour can be secured in a household where white metal is used in this way;— even lamps, lanterns, and candlesticks may share its benefits; and where lacquered metal is used for gas-fittings, bedsteads, hooks, or hanging rails, and so forth, it is important to see that the lacquer or other surface preparation is thoroughly good; for nothing makes a house look so shabby and poverty-stricken as tarnished and ill-kept metal fittings. Polished steel, once so largely used for stoves, fenders, and fire-irons, is a veritable badge of slavery to the housewife, and the time and labour required to keep them in order are worthy of a better cause. A far more beautiful and natural surface is that of iron "finished bright," by the modern method which leaves it clean and shining, but not with the smoothness of polished steel, and needing nothing but an occasional oiled rag to keep it in good condition.

Enamel is an ornament which should be very sparingly used for house decoration. A gem-like piece of colour, wisely introduced into a door-plate, lamp, or bracket, will often give great charm and distinction to the scheme in which it is set. But having once struck the keynote of

simplicity and homeliness which is proper to a
cottage, care should be taken not to adopt a
decorative method so easily vulgarised as enamel-
ling, except in sober, dignified, and congruous
surroundings. Enamel harmonises well with oak,
but not with deal, with copper or bright iron, but
not with aluminium; it demands good material,
but not elaborate detail, for its setting. Sometimes
a small enamelled panel in a cupboard door will
warm and light up a small room like a well-chosen
picture, but the cupboard in that case must be
beautiful and harmonious with the other wood-
work. On the staircase, too, a standard-lamp
or newel-post the rich glint of an enamelled
colour can be introduced; in fact the newel-post
is one of those points in the interior which may
most fittingly receive decoration—whether of
carving or added ornament; it forms, like the
fireplace, a centre of interest to the eye, and may
be adorned even lavishly, while its surroundings
are quite frugal in character, so long as there is a
basic harmony of material and colour between the
two. The heads of windows, and of the more
important doors, can also serve as points for decoration ; and there should generally be a certain cor-
respondence established between the doors and
the fireplace, as in some Queen Anne and early
Georgian houses, where the general treatment of the
opening and the style of its carvings and mouldings
are the same. Brackets or shelves over doors are

ANOTHER VIEW FROM GARDEN OF "CHERRY CROFT"

E. W. Marshall, Architect

chiefly useful to secure the rail of a curtain; they should not be encouraged as mere receptacles for china and *bric-à-brac*, and the dust that these gather around them.

It should hardly be necessary to repeat that all wood that is worth having about the house at all should be good enough to be stained and not painted. The beauty of wood is in its grain and in the texture of its surface, and anything laid upon it must be such as to reveal and emphasise these and not to efface them. The mixture known as paint in most modern house-decoration is chiefly used to cover up poor materials, and present a tolerably washable surface to the world. A simple and clean transparent stain will often be of service; but the better the quality of the wood, the less treatment will be necessary. Scrubbing should only be exacted where positively dirty work is done. Varnish is scarcely less abominable than paint; and the wood used for doors, staircases, panels, and furniture should either be good enough to stand the wear and tear of life with equanimity, or should be finished with a smooth and dull surface which can be kept in decent condition by regular rubbing with a rag, and some simple cleansing preparation which will not pretend either to give high polish or to remove inevitable scars. The application of paint to metal should be avoided as much as possible, except where tarnishable metals are exposed to

137

the open air, as in bicycles, and sometimes gates
and railings. The rule that must always be
borne in mind is, never to make one material
look like another. If metal has to be painted,
then let us see at once that it is painted metal,
and let it not pretend to be wood (as it does
when an iron bar is painted to match the shutter
to which it is attached). Similarly if the natural
grain of wood is hidden by an opaque paint, let
it be obviously paint, and not have the grain of
some other kind of wood imitated upon its
surface, as the veins of marble have often—to
our shame—been copied upon painted plaster
around the fireplaces of bygone years.

Yet it may be well just here to point out
that technical honesty of this kind is not quite
the same thing as that aggressive literalness,
studied and irritating simplicity which has become
identified with the "new art" movement of the
past ten years. The leaders of this widespread
reaction from artifice and pretence in decoration
have rushed to the opposite extreme, and have
cultivated a forced naturalness—one might almost
call it an unnatural frankness—which in its
anxiety to conceal nothing of the constructive
method, never lets us forget for a moment how
(badly very often) the thing is done. It has
even become a point of artistic honour to insist
that all wrought metal shall show the hammer
marks, and that every piece of wood construction

A THIRD VIEW FROM GARDEN OF "CHERRY CROFT"
E. W. Marshall, Architect

shall show the joints. Peculiar virtue has been attached to seams and raw edges; baldness and crudity have been read as signs of grace. Yet the great craftsmen of past ages have not been so self-conscious about these things. If their joints were apparent, well and good; but if they fell conveniently into the background, well also. No doubt the recent fashion of letting the necessary fastenings of a piece of furniture form in themselves its decoration, is in the main a good one, but it should not be carried so far that the hinge of an ordinary cupboard becomes massive enough to carry a church door. Sincerity in craftsmanship need not mean the exaggeration of practical details, and the emphasising of points which might just as easily be left quiet and unobtrusive. Truth in craftsmanship—as, indeed, in all art—does not consist in proclaiming everything, as it were, from the house-tops. It is possible to be quite satisfied that our house is well built, without always seeing the timbers that support the upper floor; nor does leaving a wooden surface entirely raw strike us as a great improvement upon the old method of polishing it by hand. It is useful as a necessary and timely protest against the artificially high polish and veneer of our childhood's days, when a table was made to shine like a mirror, which it was certainly never intended to be, and when every such article of furniture had to be protected by tiresome covers lest the immaculate surface should be scratched. We need not return to the savage and primitive in our revolt against a decadent elegance and over-refinement of this kind. Artistic sincerity consists rather in an attitude of mind which is at once open and discriminate, ready to use all materials and opportunities as they come, yet also to select and arrange them wisely, and adapt them to the purpose in hand.

Chapter XIII.—*Decoration*

IT must always be remembered that harmony between the different parts of the structure and decoration is even more important in a cottage than in a larger house; for the different parts, being nearer together, are thrown into sharper contrast, and the discrepancies that are almost sure to arise are not so easily softened down and lost sight of as when the whole scheme is carried out upon a larger scale. The various patterns brought into the same room, on textiles or flat surfaces, must be more carefully compared and selected, and greater pains must be taken that they do not clash. The number of colours must be restricted, the decorative designs restrained by masses of plain colour, and such colour properly blended with the background of the decorated materials.

It is a mistake to suppose that a large-patterned wall-paper adds apparent size to a room. It does the contrary. But there is no reason why figured designs should be banished altogether from cottage walls. A paper of small and quiet pattern, and conventional in treatment, will make an excellent background for pictures, and be entirely pleasing even in a limited space. Friezes are rarely successful in a small room, but a dado—especially of panelled wood if the money permits—helps to give an effect of spaciousness to the upper part of the room. It need hardly be said that a cottage is not the place for displaying accumulations of bric-à-brac, whether on the walls or on shelves and sideboards, nor should its entrance be "cluttered up"—as the homely housewife expresses it—by trophies of sport and ornamental heirlooms better suited to an ancestral hall.

Stencilling is a pleasant and appropriate method of decorating walls and hangings where a simple and unpretentious treatment is required. A cottage gives one of the best possible opportunities for this work, when the walls of rooms, staircase, and passages are washed, distempered, or painted instead of papered, or when a bare washed frieze surmounts the paper. The actual stencilling is easily and quickly done; the labour of the craft consists chiefly in cutting the stencils; and these, of course, once made, can be used again and again. "Home arts" have been so much abused within the last twenty years, and so discredited by amateur efforts in the way of decorative panels, screens, and so forth, that one hesitates to recommend the cottage-builder to do much of the decoration with his own hands; yet stencilling, perhaps, is the method in which the beginner, if only he have the saving grace of reticence, is least likely to go wrong. Some simple decorations in plaster may also be easily done; and we have seen some quite common kitchen fire-places redeemed from ugliness by a few strokes of the paint-brush conveying some light decorative figure in the quietest of tones, blending with the general scheme of the paint and paper. In all applied decorations, care should be taken to keep the subject-matter of the decoration in a certain congruity with its position; for instance, there is something obviously wrong in putting a representation of waves on a frieze, or close to a fire; and no less so in bringing clouds and tree-tops down into the lower part of a wall or panel. Many decorative devices have been associated for years with particular parts of the house—the stork's nest with chimneys, for example—and such traditions may just as well be adhered to in the arrangement of designs. The crowing cock has long since made his home upon the weather-vane; and many other familiar creatures have become favourite ornaments both without and within. Symbolic figures also abound, and time-honoured inscriptions, which can be adopted for decorative purposes over doors and gateways, fireplaces, and other points that readily catch the eye. Sun-dials make a delightful and romantic feature in a cottage wall or garden, and may be made in many different ways as to form and ornament. Gate lamps and lanterns are also an important feature of the exterior. They will have to be considered from the point of view of aspect and exposure to weather, care being taken that the cottage shall be easily identified in darkness by their clear and steady light. Glass of a particular colour, in harmony with the rest of the exterior, will add another note of interest and distinction to the homestead. If numbered in a row, the number of the cottage should be clearly painted, either on the lamp, or on the glass above the door, or on some part of the door where the light will clearly shine on it at night; for we all know the annoyance of tramping up and down muddy and stony bye-ways and garden-paths after an illusive No. 15, which turns out to be 45 or 4B, as the case may prove. It should not be necessary to urge that if names are adopted instead of numbers, these should be chosen which are as simple and straightforward as possible, easy to read, easy to say, and easy to remember; and not liable to be spelt in different ways. The capacities of the rural postman should not be unkindly strained by such jaw-breaking nomenclature as Llanfairfechan, Paramahatta, Bally-magrorty, and the like.

Decoration in the porch will naturally depend on its aspect and purpose—whether it be mainly a shelter in an exposed place to make the front door and its approach less bleak and inhospitable, or whether it be a sunny and pleasant place to sit in—to form a sort of summer lounge and reception room, in which case a great deal more licence may be allowed in the way of decoration and furniture. Broad fixed seats may then be put if space permit (a narrow seat is worse than none), and if a slope can be contrived for the back by means of buttresses to the wall of the porch, so much the more comfortable will it be to sit in.

It is to be assumed that the country cottage will not afford much scope for the laying out of grounds and flower-beds, though indeed a skilled gardener will often achieve wonders of leaf and blossom within a few feet of his walls. Sometimes, however, all that can be done will be to make a gravel path from the gate to the front door, with a grass plot on either side, and perhaps a row of trees within the boundary wall. It will add considerably to the charm of the entrance if the path is of brick on edge laid longitudinally, or in some pattern such as herring-bone. Another pleasant arrangement is to place single bricks end in in the form of some repeating pattern and filling in between with small pebble, flint, or even flags cut to the shape required. Efforts in the direction of hedging will only be repaid if based on a careful observance of what shrubs grow well in the neighbourhood, and of what is already there in the way of a hedge or a bank. Nothing is more delightful than an old hospitable hedge into which all sorts of flowery visitants have strayed in the course of generations,—sweet-briar and wild roses, honeysuckle and convolvulus, attaching themselves to the more solid and abiding hawthorn or other bush. One of the first things

that strikes the visitor from foreign countries is
the beauty of our English hedgerows, not only
the thick-set growths that flank the country lane,
but even the little boundary shrubs that divide
field from garden; "hardly hedgerows"—as
Wordsworth says—"little lines of sportive wood
run wild." Evergreen bushes have a charm of
their own, but the hedge that reflects the
changing seasons is perhaps to be generally
preferred. In setting this, provision must be
made for the winter season, and its growth must
be sturdy enough to make a hedge when the
twigs are bare.

In fences also local peculiarities may be
observed; and there are probably as many
pleasing ways of placing boards and rails in
fencing as there are of shaping and arranging
the slender balusters of an indoor balustrade.
Obviously, strength or security are of the first
importance, but lightness is desirable from the
standpoint of expense. If wood is used it must
be well seasoned, and it may either be left to
improve its surface by weather, or it may be
tarred or painted. Low boundary walls of stone
and flint belong properly to certain districts, and
their sober and somewhat cold look makes a
perfect background for the colouring of holly-
hocks and gillyflowers.

In the case of model villages and communal
settlements a great deal can be done in the

way of laying out greens and quadrangles to harmonise with the general spirit of the architecture. The estate will probably have its own ponds and stream, avenues, garden-plots, playing fields, and bowling-green, with rustic bridges where required, and a modest bandstand for the summer. But no attempt at formal gardening should be made where the cottages are homely and pastoral in character. Attempts to combine the ceremonial and courtly style with the rural and archaic will never please the sensitive eye. The developments of the next few years may bring, perchance, the " garden village " as well as the " garden city " within habitable reach of the ordinary citizen; but success will depend on the building being done sincerely and unpretentiously to fulfil a genuine need, and not in the spirit of the modern " restorer " who recently showed the present writers a house which had been under his care, saying proudly, " You see this was built as an Italian villa, but *we've made it Tudor* ! " Not by such means shall be regained the comfort and beauty of an English cottage home.

Index

Index

UNIFORM WITH THIS VOLUME

The Country Handbooks

A Series of Illustrated Practical Handbooks dealing with Country Life, suitable for the Pocket or Knapsack

Under the General Editorship of
HARRY ROBERTS

Price 3s. net. bound in Limp Cloth.
Price 4s. net. bound in Limp Leather.

An Eight-page Prospectus Post Free on Application.

BOOKS ABOUT GARDENS

TWO ILLUSTRATED CLASSICS

By GILBERT WHITE

THE NATURAL HISTORY OF SEL-BORNE. Edited, with Introduction, by GRANT ALLEN. With upwards of 200 Illustrations by EDMUND H. NEW.

Price 5s. net.   Crown 8vo.

"The attraction lies chiefly in finding the masterpiece so admir-ably illustrated by Mr Edmund H. New. In black and white line work of this class he has no equal."—*Country Life.*

"Mr Edmund New's drawings are not merely artistic, but full of the poetry of association."—*Speaker.*

"We have never seen this book in a more agreeable or ap-propriate form."—*St James's Gazette.*

By IZAAK WALTON AND CHARLES COTTON

THE COMPLEAT ANGLER. Edited, with an Introduction, by RICHARD LE GALLIENNE. With Photogravure Portraits of Walton and Cotton, and over 250 Illustrations and Cover-design by EDMUND H. NEW.

Price 15s. net.   Fcap. 4to.

"A delightful edition, charmingly illustrated."—*Punch.*

"Of Mr Edmund H. New's illustrations we cannot speak too highly. We have never seen better."—*Spectator.*

"One of the best editions; one, we cannot help thinking, that Walton himself would have preferred."—*Daily Chronicle.*

"A beautiful edition of Isaac Walton's immortal work. The great charm of the new edition is Mr New's illustrations. They are beautiful reproductions of surface sketches which are in complete harmony with the spirit of Arcadian peace, characteristic of the grand old angler's pages."—*The Pall Mall Gazette.*

"This is the most delightful form that 'The Compleat Angler' has ever taken."—*The Globe.*

Printed in the USA
CPSIA information can be obtained
at www.ICGtesting.com
LVHW021126181223
766763LV00012B/653